The Edge of the Volcano
And Other Journeys

The Edge of the Volcano
And Other Journeys

MICHEL
GAUTHIER

EDEN BOOKS

An Eden Books Production
Pattaya, Thailand
Copyright © 2013 Michel Gauthier
All rights reserved.
ISBN: 9798844132520

CONTENTS

Africa

Slaying Dragons.. 9

The World in the Molishi 32

The Rebel, the Dynamite and the Fish 36

The Flies 46

The Edge of the Volcano.. 50

Arabia

Hamdan the Ghost Horse 61

The Taking of VW3 65

The Mauve Ghost (A Libyan Tale)............................. 71

The Catch 75

Missed 81

Triple-Cross... 85

Europe

The Cemetery of the Elephants 130

Naphthalene Must Be Banned 134

Hard Luck 136

The Meeting 138

Dinner 142

The Shaft 144

Asia

The Journeys of the Butterflies 158

Betrayals 198

John Was Here 202

The Pilgrimage 204

Glossary 219

About the Author 221

AFRICA

SLAYING DRAGONS

Fairy tales are a fraud. Not so much because of dragons; dragons do exist and I have eyeballed some. I have also slain a couple, although not of the larger species. No, the fraud is in the aftermath. Every dragon slayer will know that once out of the cave and looking for the thereafter of bliss, the horse in actual life is irretrievably lame, the rented suit of armor is so battered that the agency wants to charge the full replacement price and the maiden is a hunchback with children born from other fathers holding her skirts. This is the fraud and the toughest part of life. This true story is for all of us who would have been better off leaving alone the dragons in their souls.

*

On that gloomy, greyish November day in the Ardennes I was licking my wounds at my parents' house, assessing the financial damage caused by a long escape across Africa, and putting a brave face on it for not even a hunchback was bothering about me. Mr and Mrs Smets had insisted on coming to visit me, despite the long journey in the rain. Their black cloaks had the smell of wet clothes. Distress was visible on their pale, austere faces. My mother had introduced them in the damp, chilly lounge, had served coffee and retreated to the warm kitchen. I was left with the parents of my friend.

The questions were predictable: you were with Mark shortly before he disappeared. His last letter is dated 20 July. Do you know what happened to him? When did you see him last? What was he doing? Do you think he may be alive?

The sadness, the despair, the hopelessness were overwhelming. I wanted to help, to share, to comfort, and yet, knowing the answers or some of them, I couldn't really speak. What I knew of the fate of Mark Smets wasn't really speakable, and definitely not to his grieving parents. I uttered a few innocuous generalities, gave vague irrelevant details and—most cowardly of all—denied knowledge of the essential. The sight of their black, stooped shoulders as they left through the door into the rain will haunt me forever, together with the events that took place in Kindu a few months earlier. Perhaps I should have told them and we should have cried together.

*

That night in late July I had been asleep for a couple of hours when the rattle of several vehicles stopping in the driveway shook the windows of the bungalow. I walked with blinking eyes to the door on the terraced porch. Traffic was non-existent at that time of the night in our mining outpost, lost deep in Africa. If some drinking had been going on, I would have been part of it. Clearly, this was an unusual event. Uniformed silhouettes emerged from the darkness and I recognized Mark Smets, commander of the first company of the tenth "Kansimba" commando battalion.

Mark was an old pal. Young, short, somewhat round with curly hair, he was forever cheerful and optimistic. He endlessly whistled the Beatles' *Yellow Submarine* tune. We would dine and drink together every once in a while, swapping dreams and plans for a better, funnier world. Until today my throat is taut and I have difficulty swallowing when I hear the silly melody.

But we had not reached that stage yet. Mark walked in with most of his staff: my friend Louis, the failed priest and repentant veteran of the Flemish Legion; the tall Giancarlo, a handsome and self-conscious petty thief from Milano; Perrin, a young French professional soldier; Marcel, a tense offspring of the Brussels underworld; and a couple of mustachioed Afrikaaners. They all carried weapons and bandoliers. A couple had hand grenades hanging from their belts. First things first: I handed them beers before asking questions. Alerted by the commotion, a couple of neighbors joined in and we had an awkward party going.

But then Mark explained.

The dawn of a new era was with us. The savior, appropriately named Moise (Moses in English) Tshombe had risen from the ashes of his political ruin two years before. Now every warrior of his native Katanga province had rallied to the banner of Tshombe's new liberal and friendly Congo. The enemy was the low life Armée Nationale Congolaise—ANC in short and for cursing—of double-tongued usurper Mobutu.

The French mercenaries of Bob Denard's 6th Battalion had joined the uprising. Coordinated troops were now attacking simultaneously Kisangani, Bukavu and Kindu. Mark was here with his fierce Kansimba soldiers to conquer Kindu. He had left the Punia barracks in the afternoon and planned to pounce on the provincial capital at dawn the next day. He had stopped at our little place for refreshment, to say hi, and to discuss a little technicality.

Kindu was a small city of perhaps ten thousand Africans and a hundred foreigners. The mighty Lualaba river separated the right bank, with its Transaco warehouses and villages, from the heart of town. On the opposite bank were the airport, capable of handling C130 airplanes, the military camp housing the ANC's infamous 21st Infantry Battalion, the "Hotel du Relais" — where weary half-cast and white survivors met arrogant local upstarts — the post office and the church.

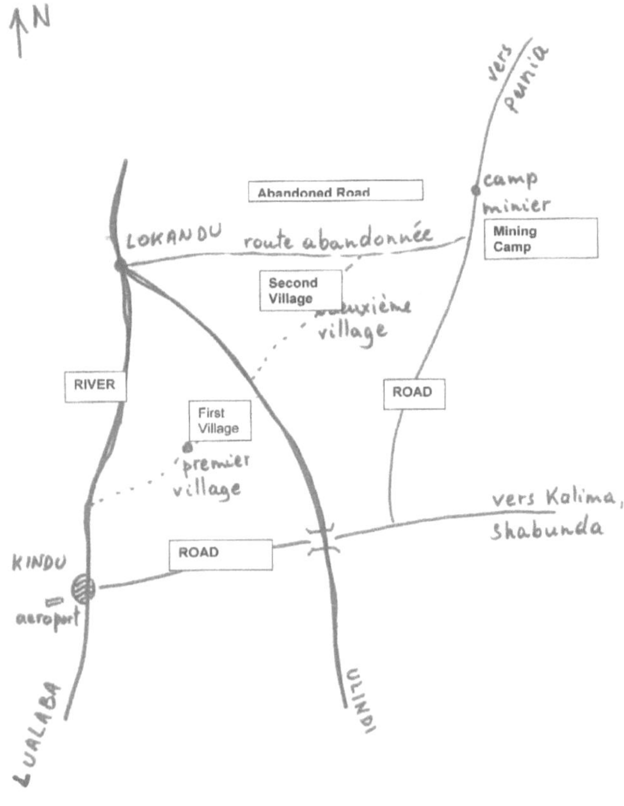

To get from the Transaco bank, from where Mark's assault had to be launched, to the left bank one mile away, one had to use the ferry or one's own craft. At night, the ferry was on the left bank, the wrong one from Mark's perspective.

The turnaround time of the diesel-operated barge was about half an hour. Naturally, the appearance of Mark's invading column of eight jeeps bristling with machine guns and six lorries packed with fighters would make the crew of the ferry somewhat jittery and they would shy from extending their services. Besides, the invaders, if identified beforehand and caught on the ferry, would be an easy target for the 21st. So the Kansimba battalion supplied its first company with a number of assault craft for a stealth crossing before dawn.

Mark's technicality wasn't that he was attacking a full-sized battalion across a large river with a single company. In fact his single company of less than one hundred men was going to attack not one but two battalions since the third commando battalion of the ANC had recently been sent to Kindu, possibly following leaks in Tshombe's environment.

But nobody knew that at the time. The Kansimbas were brave in their own way and, had they known, they probably would still have gone in. No, Mark's problem was more serious: somehow, the outboard engines of the assault craft had remained in Punia… At that point of the explanations, we heard a rifle shot in the distance.

"Don't worry," said Mark, "this will be Jacques mopping up the police station."

As it was, the single report had signaled the shooting of a lonely, destitute and unarmed policeman manning the Territory Administration in our isolated resort. The sudden reality of war and death cast a spell on our group, whilst the aberration of the present killing produced sourness and tightness in my throat.

Mark was all business and not thrown off his mission. "Have you got oars?" said he. He didn't laugh. The other mercenaries were serious and concerned. For a while, my neighbors and I remained speechless at the colossal ineptitude of the situation. There were no oars in the lounge, or in the kitchen, or in the bedroom. For Chrissake, we were mining engineers: we sweated it out in the jungle all day and when we had a break, we drank beer and sang wild songs; we didn't go rowing on bloody canals, of which there were none around there anyway.

For a long while we pondered the situation: the missing outboards, the first company here two hundred kilometers away from Punia and eighty kilometers short of Kindu, the dead policeman, the rest of the Kansimba battalion about to attack Kisangani in the North and Bukavu in the East, the beer running out and getting warm in our glasses. Restless feet and chairs scraped on the cement floor. The night was warm and sticky. We all sweated. My stock of beer being exhausted on account of the number of visitors, I produced a couple of bottles of brandy and we drank another round in muted incredulity. Louis was clearly distressed at the mess.

One of my dragons chose that moment of obtuse meditation to raise its foolish head. My lonely childhood had been enriched by the tales of gallant heroes of old, of Buffalo Bill, Michel Ney and Lancelot. I had never wondered if I would be brave under fire and, not having been a soldier, had left a longing in my uneducated soul. As an engineer I had at the same time a taste for intellectual challenges and a love of logic. Clearly this was a case to indulge in both—a test of courage and ingenuity in the face of careless logistics and adverse circumstances.

"Suppose there was a known civilian in a known, harmless Land-Rover—say, like myself—followed by an anonymous truck, covered in tarp and loaded with hidden Kansimbas. They approach the landing at dawn and call for the ferry to pick them up? The ferry crew recognizes routine business and crosses the Lualaba. As the ferry touches the

Transaco bank, the Kansimbas get off their Trojan truck and seize the barge. We cross the river and establish a bridge head on the left bank. The rest of the column joins in and gets to the left bank with the secured ferry, under the protection of the bridgehead."

As I spoke I knew I was an idiot.

Sure enough, before I closed my mouth and grabbed a glass of brandy, Mark approved of my plan. Little practicalities were agreed in no time: who goes in which vehicle, which platoon to assign to the covered truck and what schedule to follow. Louis had been around these parts many years as a farmer and then as the head of security for our mine. He was well known around here and deemed harmless, so he would ride with me to implement the little ploy.

Despite my semi-dazed state, what with the awakening in the middle of the night and the unexpected hosting, I could see that Mark was breathing a huge sigh of relief. I had a deep sense of doom at my irrepressible tendency to step forward out of sync and out of reason. But it was already too late and I was committed.

We rolled out of the settlement. Louis had joined me in the Land-Rover and we drove ahead of the first company, with the notion that our harmless civilian appearance would be a tripwire in case of trouble ahead. As we left the mining post we passed by the body of the policeman. To all intents and purposes that was a murder. Louis didn't disagree but didn't offer any worthwhile justification. I was mad at them and at myself in a hollow, helpless and ineffective way.

The warm and sticky atmosphere of the bungalow had disappeared. We shivered in the cool wind of the drive. We passed the bridge on the Ulindi river, a powerful tributary of the Lualaba. The river had generated a ghostly mist, and for a while we travelled in a detached world of our own, with no destination, no beginning and no end. But our plans loomed in front of us. We didn't talk and smoked cigarette after cigarette. The lethal swirls of the "Albert Bleues" filled the cabin of the Land-Rover. The French "Gauloises" are ladies' stuff in comparison to the "Albert". An "Albert Bleue" kills mosquitoes at twenty feet. Smoking gave an illusion of warmth.

By 5am, we were at the agreed stand-by position for the column of the first company. We had a final conference with Mark and Louis. The sky hinted at daybreak and there was no further escape: the dragon had stirred in its sleep and the fear was biting at my bowels. Louis Otten and I drove on to the ferry landing, with the Trojan truck scheduled about five minutes behind us. Approaching the godowns of Transaco, we overtook a growing crowd of early workers walking to their tasks. As we stopped at the landing, I flashed the lights of the Land-Rover and a minute later we saw the crew getting the ferry under way from the left bank. We watched the slow-moving barge with clenched jaws and tight fists. The Trojan truck stopped behind us. As the driver killed the engine, the silence screamed. The ferry seemed to take forever to arrive.

When it finally did, the crewmen jumped in the water and lashed the chains to the bollards in the tall grass. I walked casually to the back of the truck and knocked on the sideboards, whispering in an excited voice, "Kuja! Upesi!" At my injunction, the Kansimbas, their assault rifles at the ready, threw back the tarp and filed out of their hiding place. The crewmen looked at the other bank. It was too far to swim back and they cooperated right away. Louis took half of the platoon across the river to establish a bridgehead. Good luck,

Louis, I thought as I went back to report and fetch Mark with the rest of the column.

The drive lasted five minutes and a life time. Alone on the road, alone to possess the knowledge of what was happening at either and both ends, I felt an enormous rush of adrenaline. My heartbeat was fast and my mind raced between God Almighty and the Avenging Angels. As I reached the waiting column, I did a flying U-turn, shouting at Mark that we had done it. In my excitement, I drove again towards the landing, ahead of the troops as an awkward vanguard made up of an unlikely lone warrior in tee-shirt and shorts.

The first company rolled behind at its convoy speed and in my haste I pulled away. Torn between the desire to get back to the ferry and the safety of remaining with the troops, I hovered a couple of hundred meters ahead of the point jeep like a young, untrained shepherd dog. At the landing, the ferry was back and Louis was safely entrenched on the other bank. Mark congratulated me and immediately assigned crossing priorities and targets. Soldiers were milling about and sections were assembled on the ferry for the trip.

Suddenly idle, I pondered what to do and, spurred by a restless dragon or unwavering fate, I volunteered to stick around and cross with the Kansimbas. I was assigned an assault rifle, the famed Belgian 7.62-caliber Fal, with one magazine of twenty rounds. I left the gun on the back of a jeep during the crossing and when we disembarked, the magazine had disappeared: prudent soldiers keep their pockets full of ammo. Mark shouted and someone handed me another magazine.

Now the attacking sections were formed. Louis, beaming from his bridgehead success, together with Perrin, Giancarlo and the Afrikaaners would follow the Lualaba to the right, take the military camp and wipe out its garrison of the 21st ANC battalion. Mark, Marcel, Jacques and their platoons were moving straight ahead away from the river to secure the airport. Mark assigned me to a section of Kansimbas under Adjutant Leonard, with the task of taking the headquarters of the 21st, located in a residential villa. We progressed at an angle, between Louis' column to our right and Mark's to our left. Both columns had jeeps with mounted machine guns. They drove slowly away with skirmishers on foot fanning ahead and on the flanks. Our little group was on foot and in a few minutes we were alone.

We were in the residential area of Kindu. The villas were surrounded by lawns, decorative shrubs, bushes of flowers, palm trees, eucalyptus and laurels. The houses were silent and unfriendly. Grey clouds were hanging low and the chill of the early hours wasn't gone. We walked up a steepish hill, moving through the gardens. Spurred on by my personal hydra but with knotted guts, I placed myself at the front of our little group, abreast with Leonard.

Rifle and machine gun fire erupted to our right: Louis was engaging the 21st. The rattle was distant and did not give a sense of immediate threat. Then an ear-splitting burst of automatic weapon exploded right behind me. I literally jumped out of my socks and turned around to see a fretful Kansimba firing his Fal right at my heels, in support of his comrades now steadily shooting to our distant right. To hell with displaying gusto, I decided to walk at the back of our little band. The section opened up and more shooting thundered through the landscape. One Kansimba started limping in front of me and leaned to examine a bullet graze in his lower leg. Although I was somewhat rattled by the emerging confusion and commotion, I suspected he might have been hit by an overenthusiastic colleague.

Before I knew it we were in the garden of the 21st's headquarters. Leonard told me that there were only two opposition soldiers here and that they had fled. I wondered how in hell he knew that, but then realized I had to allow for being a beginner in the game of war, and for being seriously out of my depth at that particular moment.

There was a lull; everything stalled. No one seemed to know where to go from here. We looked idly at discarded reports from the 21st battalion on the floor of their abandoned HQ. We were saved from making a decision: a Kansimba ran in, breathing fast. Louis was stuck against solid positions. There was no way he could progress, let alone make an impression on the retrenched 21st. So much for our strategy. Now Louis retreated towards the ferry landing and sent a runner to tell us to fall back with him. Leonard's men entered the villa once again for a final loot and we walked downhill.

An asphalt road ran parallel to the Lualaba, about two or three hundred meters away. Along the road, the shops and warehouses were closer to each other than the villas on the hill and formed a corridor to funnel traffic and action. Now Louis and his men were between the road and the river bank. Leonard, our half dozen of Kansimbas and I were stranded between two buildings on the wrong side of the road. A machine gun of the 21st was enfilading the road and crossing it in open view of the gunner would have been dangerous. One by one the Kansimbas and Leonard made a dash for the relative safety of Louis' side and after a short while I was alone.

Adventures are made of endless waiting. Nothing much happened. Bullets flew in the street but were harmless as long as I stayed behind the gable of the store which gave me shelter. My respite however couldn't last long and soon I had to move. My throat was tight and my tummy was getting liquid. A voice somewhere in the bushes behind the store shouted, "Avancez kuna!" in a mixture of French and Lingala. This was 21st stuff, frighteningly close. I had to do something. John, the tallest, thinnest and coolest of the three South Africans was crouching behind the corner of a house opposite me in the street. I shouted to him in broken English for covering fire in the street. As he emptied the magazine of his Fal in the general direction of the machine gun, I made my run. My legs moved in cotton wool. My muscles had no power. The Fal in my right hand weighed a ton and upset my balance. The street was endlessly wide. I was out of breath. I was scared. And then I reached safety and collapsed behind John, out of reach of the machine gun and of the bad guys progressing in the bushes.

I had a war council with Louis; the prognosis wasn't good. The 21st soldiers I overheard in the bushes had now cut off Mark and his group. They had also outflanked our left and we were just about surrounded with our back to the river. We still had the ferry but the landing was under fire and so exposed that it was now a deathtrap. Louis was a nice guy, but he wasn't a commander. He wasn't Zorro or John Wayne or Rambo. So we waited near the corner from where John had provided covering fire for my crossing. We lay in a shallow drainage ditch. Most Kansimbas were scattered, holding a loose perimeter in a casual, desultory manner which reeked of surrender and desertion. The low clouds had finally burned out under the sun and an oppressive heat clamped everything under a mantle of warm dampness. But the sun wasn't yet bright. It may have been 11am at that point.

Now the 21st had another machine gun in position to our left. It covered the ferry landing and pinned us down. Our little group included John and the other South Africans, Louis, Perrin, Giancarlo and a couple of Kansimbas. We kept our heads below the rim of the ditch. From time to time the machine gun fired a burst which would leave a dotted line of pock marks on the wall behind us. The dotted lines got lower and lower. The sense of doom was palpable.

Out of nowhere, Leonard, the section leader who took us to the 21st's HQ, appeared and walked along the wall under the dotted lines. At this very moment the machine gun opened up again and I observed over my right shoulder a line of impacts at groin height starting from the corner and catching up with Leonard. As the impacts reached him he fell to the ground. The line continued in a crash of flying dust and cement debris. I felt a strong blow at the back of my right thigh. In the commotion I assessed I had witnessed my first war casualty and I was afraid to look at Leonard's body. I wished I had left my dragons alone.

Then Leonard stood up with an enormous grin on his face. He had seen death coming and he had cheated it. Well, good for him, but our situation was as precarious as ever. The blow on my leg was from a flying brick fragment. It bled a bit but nothing to worry about. Louis and the others had a war council: time to retreat if we still could. We fired a volley and ran into the waste land between the asphalt road and the Lualaba bank. Now the sun had started biting and we were sweating. We crossed a deep ditch with difficulty and then crawled through tall grass to keep a low profile. At this point I bitterly regretted my casual clothing: no one in his right mind would ever crawl in short sleeves. In no time my elbows were cut up by sharp leaves and angular stones. I tried to worm my way on my tummy without the help of my elbows. My progress went from bad to worse and I fell behind our group at an alarming rate. Thank God we reached the river bank and the nature of our ordeal changed. How could we get back to the safety of the right bank?

Several godowns were built along the river edge. One had a jetty and — thank you, God, for this miracle — a moored tug boat. The craft was a flat boat built in the manner of the show boats of the Mid-West USA, but without the paddle wheels. We ran under the intermittent bursts of the machine gun and found — second miracle — that the boat captain was on board. We crowded over him and he had no choice. He started the engine. To our horror, however, we didn't move. John, yet again the coolest of us, observed that we were still tied up to the jetty. A brief and furious exchange took place to decide who would jump out of the boat to unleash the moorings. Eventually Jack, the short South African, made the run under thickening fire. His mates watched us impassively, as if daring us to leave without him. Jack eventually made it and we were on the move.

As the shore receded, one hundred, then two hundred meters away, then half a mile in agonizing slow motion, an overwhelming sense of relief made us talk loud and fast and laugh at our recent unspoken fright. We were alive and young and the sun was shining and gave warmth. We counted ourselves: Louis, Perrin, Giancarlo, John, Jack, Dick, the old one with a limp, two Kansimbas and the boat captain. We wondered what became of Mark, Marcel and the other soldiers of 1st Company. To keep our conscience at bay we confirmed to each other that they still had control of the ferry and could possibly attempt their own crossing.

The base truth was that we were powerless, we were running away and Mark with his team were on their own, surrounded and left to their fate. As for ourselves we reckoned it was safer to take the tug boat downstream till we reached the city of Lokandu, about 30km away on the right bank, and from where an old road would lead us back to the mining camp.

We, or rather the captain, set a course skirting the right bank. We started recovering mentally from the debacle. The left bank and its looming threats were far away. Suddenly a rattle like a hail downpour shattered our tranquility. Puzzled, we looked around. There was a string of splashes crossing the Lualaba in a straight line pointing at us. A machine gun was firing and the impacts on the water, stitch-like, worked better for the gunner than any tracers! We were the proverbial sitting ducks on this slow tug boat. Every burst of fire was hitting the boat.

There was genuine unadulterated panic. We all scampered for cover. With an engineering eye, I picked up a recess between a sturdy winch and the starboard gunwale, keeping the bulk of the winch and the thickness of its two steel flanges between the machine gun and myself. Lying on my back I saw bullets splintering the wooden floor above me. I hoped fervently that the helmsman, John again, was still alive and at the wheel. Then the fire subsided and stopped. We stood up and looked at each other in bewilderment of being alive and unhurt. John came down from the upper deck, swearing profusely as only few gifted Anglo-Saxons can. A bullet had smacked into the edge of the bench on which he was sitting to steer the boat. He proclaimed he wasn't going to do it any longer. Louis somehow convinced the boat captain to take the helm and we were all secretly thankful. By then, it was three or four pm and, having been on the move since midnight, I had become hopelessly thirsty. I explored the boat and found a kitchen on the upper deck with a promising aluminium water filter. A bullet had pierced the body of the container just above the bottom and the contents had leaked on the floor. There wasn't a drop of drinking water on the cursed boat.

Then a loud whack echoed across the expanse of water: an unexpectedly beautiful geyser of water erupted about one hundred meters away at eight o'clock. My exhausted mind took a couple of seconds to translate the pretty sight into the acknowledgement that we were under mortar fire. Another machine gun opened up and I resumed my sheltering position near the winch, watching a couple of mortar rounds splashing around.

Again, the commotion receded and we looked at each other. Louis and I stood up on the protected starboard side of the boat and started a private war council when a deafening burst of automatic rifle fire jolted us into a desperate run for our lives. I dove back into my favorite recess between the winch and the gunwale. A ricochet bounced against the flange of the winch and died in front of me after hitting the gunwale. I picked up the distorted metal piece and burned my fingers. I threw the short lived (or was it the near death) souvenir into the Lualaba and turned around to see how Louis had fared. He was crumpled, moaning on the deck behind me. Perrin appeared out of nowhere and already had an open pack of dressings to tend to Louis' bullet wound in the arm. Perrin also readied a syringe of morphine and stabbed Louis in the thigh. We then discussed what happened and came to the obvious conclusion that a lone soldier of the 21st must have crossed to the right back of the Lualaba, to buy fish from villagers or whatever, and had emptied his automatic rifle in our general direction. Our sense of panic and total vulnerability was multiplied beyond breaking point.

Almost without discussion, we grounded the boat on the right shore near a footpath visible in the steep embankment and abandoned ship without another thought. The sudden silence was deafening: no more engine, no machine gun, no mortar, no shouting. We looked around and took stock. Our resources were scant: weapons and little ammo, two pangas with the Afrikaaners, the first aid pack with Perrin, some melted chocolate and soggy chewing gum with Giancarlo.

Louis was in shock from the wound, dazed by the morphine and not quite capable of proceeding under his own power. The Kansimbas and the Afrikaaners used the pangas to cut young trees and make a rough stretcher with vines. The exercise took about half an hour. It was 5pm when we got on the way up the bank. Four of us carried the stretcher on our shoulders. The crude timber crushed the flesh and in no time it became unbearable. The slope was very steep and muddy. We slipped backwards and swore. The stretcher swayed like a drunken boat in rapids. Louis, either out of fright or as a result of re-emerging consciousness, stood up and decided to walk. We were too exhausted to argue and we thankfully fell in line. I walked behind Louis and noticed drops of blood on the grass along the track. My despair at the situation was almost total: tiredness, thirst, hunger, lack of resources, no workable plan; doom was inevitable. The gradient was murderous and the weight of the Fal alone was sufficient to crush me. However, we got to the top of the incline and the level track on soft, even ground restored a modicum of confidence in our ghostlike company. As the shadows of the early evening seeped through the tall trees we reached an isolated village in the forest.

There might have been about twenty huts in the place, roughly distributed in two parallel rows on either side of a sort of main street. Each hut had its own garden or livestock pen surrounded by a palisade, a lupangu in the local dialect. A few natives, unaware of the commotion in Kindu but weary of our intrusion, provided food and water. We were so destitute that we wolfed down anything and everything with little regard for the status of our hosts. My status in the group, however, rose to the top since I was the only one, with Louis, to speak Swahili.

The villagers put a hut at our disposal and, after a hasty council to agree on the rotation of guard duties, I lay down on a reed mat and instantly fell asleep. I had slept for two minutes or so it seemed when Perrin shook me: my guard was from midnight to one o'clock. I hated the interruption of my sleep and the night was cold. I shivered in the ghostly mist. The moon was bright and cast an eerie illumination in main street, where I walked up and down, looking at my watch every minute in the hope that I could go back to my mat. I was uneasy as well, feeling responsible for our little sleeping band, for Louis' helplessness and having little clue as to how to handle this mess. I had overheard Giancarlo suggest that we leave Louis in this village and proceed only with valid hands.

I cheated by five minutes and woke John up too early. He protested but I was asleep before he finished his admonitions. About two minutes later or so it seemed again, Jack shook me, saying that something was happening in the village. It was now 5am. Jack had heard voices and whispers, shuffling noises of moving creatures. I silently followed him to the main street and at once I could hear a faint rattle in all directions. The population was fleeing. We worried that an ambush might be prepared for our little exposed band.

I walked with Jack at the back of the lupangus on the right side of the main street. A back door creaked as we approached. My Fal was level at my right hip and, as an old man passed through the door, he literally walked into the barrel of the rifle.

"Unakwenda wapi?" Where are you going? The man shuddered. He carried a panga in one hand and a case in the other. An elderly woman was behind him with a large bundle wrapped in a piece of cloth balanced on her head. He was one of the very last inhabitants of this godforsaken hamlet who had not yet fled. I convinced him easily that he should stay with our group to guide us out of the forest and towards the mining camp. With the villager under close watch, we had a hasty breakfast of bananas under the rising sun and another war council. Backed up by Dick, the oldest of the Afrikaaners and supposedly a veteran of Monte Cassino, Giancarlo openly voiced his suggestion to abandon Louis. Perrin and I disagreed. Our little band was incapacitated without someone able to converse with the natives. I had become an important person in our microcosm and my word carried weight. The issue was settled in the style "one for all and all for one" but a grudge lingered in the air.

In the village we were bottled in an inverted V between the Lualaba to our left and the Ulindi to our right and front. To reach the mines we had to march to the north-east and cross the Ulindi river. Our reluctant guide agreed to take us to the bank of the Ulindi and we got going. An easy trek of about one hour, guide and elderly lady walking point, took us to the river bank. The water was a quarter of a mile wide. The flow was slow. There were four rotting dugouts on the shore. Each had several holes in the hull. The reluctant guide discovered a paddle in the bushes. He must have been laughing at our predicament. Then Jack, yet again the do-er, pushed the canoes in the water and, mixing clay in his hands, proceeded to plug the worst of the leaks.

Under the pressure of our no-choice situation, we imitated him and embarked on a type of raft, each passenger holding onto the gunwale of the adjacent canoe. I found myself with one hand on the canoe to the right, one heel pressing on the clay plug of a leak and my left hand pressing on another. We had to let go of the guide and his lady and he had disappeared in a flash. Jack had the one paddle and he steered us across the river towards a landing point indicated by the villager.

The crossing took long enough for me to suffer from repeated cramps, the result of our awkward positions. The bizarre and precarious navigation wasn't conducive of great spirits. Our flotilla was incongruous, unwieldy and fragile. We progressed slowly at the pace of Jack's paddling. John alternated with Jack every ten minutes or so. Thank God, the crossing was over before any of our "mutumbu" was in real danger of sinking. The sudden relief of standing on terra firma again, of having a clear track in front of us, was overwhelming. Even Louis walked tall despite his wound. Perrin was at his side. We walked at a leisurely pace for most of the day on a level track. The going wasn't hard and we covered good ground.

By late afternoon, we reached a large village. The headmen were knowledgeable and wise people. They understood the situation and saw the wisdom of helping us. How did we look important rather than destitute and helpless? I couldn't really figure that out, but then they were the wise guys and we still ostentatiously held eight automatic rifles between us.

The wise villagers brought a feast of rice and fried chickens, sombe, bananas and papayas. We wolfed down the food in a riot of joy and relief at being alive and, for the time being, out of harm's way. Then the sun sank below the dense foliage and we settled down for the night. Perrin insisted on another hourly guard routine and I inherited again the midnight to one am duty. With a happy stomach I collapsed into deep sleep and resented the wake up call. I slowly got up in the middle of the night and, the Fal on my shoulder, started pacing the large village plaza. The stress of the past thirty-six hours was heavy on my youthful resilience. A large fire was dying down in the middle of the common. A native deck chair was invitingly laid out next to the fire. I was tired and shivering in the damp, cold night. I sat in the deck chair, having rationalized my weakness as a short break between two walks around the plaza. Before I knew it I was asleep and woke up at half-past one. Thoroughly embarrassed, I shook Jack who had the one to two am watch. I was very annoyed with myself, quite aware that a sentry found asleep in wartime is usually shot. I let my people down. God knew what could have happened during my dereliction of responsibility. Jack had a knowing look on his face. I pretended all was A-OK and I was just carried away so that I kind of over-sentried. End of argument. I couldn't care less anyway. I wanted to sleep and I collapsed again in the hut.

In the morning, some fifty hours after Mark Smets' intrusive stopover at my place, we resumed the trek towards the mining camp. Again the going wasn't too rough and became easier as we reached the old road from Lokandu. Because of rotten and broken bridges, the road was used only by pedestrians.

We made good progress. By 10am we reached the main road from Punia to Kindu. The mining camp couldn't be far away to our left. We had a break and a chat on the grassy embankment. Dick and Louis were worn out and wanted to stay there until help came. John, Giancarlo and Jack would keep them company. The one Kansimba still with us decided to try his chance by himself—without our conspicuous company—and disappeared into the foliage. That left Perrin and me. We both disliked passivity. We decided to carry on towards the mining camp, hoping it would still be in friendly hands.

So we proceeded, Perrin to the right and I on the left, Fal at the ready. The road was quiet. Very quiet. We reached the village with the Territory Administrative Office where the policeman had been shot two nights before. Not a soul, not a dog, not a chicken. The deserted place gave us the creeps. It was also scary because the natives always scamper in case of trouble. What trouble was there ahead? Were we the trouble? Had the ANC overtaken us on the main road during the two days of our trek in the forest? Thankfully the body of the policeman had been removed. We were now between the village and the mining camp, on an isolated stretch of road, encased between two vertical cuts of some ten feet on either side. This two or three hundred meters portion of road was thus like a dry gully with nowhere to go except forward or backward. We were in the middle of it when we heard the rumble of an engine in front of us. The vehicle was approaching fast. Our heartbeats revved right away.

ANC or good guys? Where to hide?

Miraculously again, a narrow drain through the vertical road bank opened up to my left and in one step I was out of view. I curled into the vegetation and glanced back towards the road. Perrin was literally levitating up the vertical right bank of the road and rolled over the edge, out of sight of the approaching truck which now roared down the empty gully. As it flashed past, I saw green berets on the flat bed. Kansimbas! These were the rear echelon left behind at the mining camp by Mark Smets two nights ago. Thank you, God! Perrin rolled down from his perch and I jumped back on the road, waving wildly at the back of the truck. They saw us; they stopped; we embraced each other.

"No, the ANC is not here!" The camp was quiet and waiting for the news. The camp was so near that the truck dropped us before going out to collect Louis, Giancarlo and the Afrikaaners.

I had a long bath in my bungalow and found I'd contracted dysentery from the water drunk in the jungle. The dysentery would have the best of me for the following two months.

After a long journey, I would evade the ANC and get back to Belgium to another career and another life. For a while, however, I would have bad dreams and I would shudder at backfiring cars.

*

As for the aftermath, the news in the area was that Mark Smets and his guys had been captured. His body had been dismembered by exulting soldiers. Bits and pieces were displayed in Kindu, Kalima and Shabunda. It was reported that some victors of the 21st battalion had feasted on his flesh. I do not know how he died. I hope it was quick and that his parents never knew the details.

Louis recovered, escaped and eventually opened a furniture shop in Oostende. We got very drunk when I visited him a couple of years later. Perrin, my friend, wherever you are, I hope you're well.

Myself, I still occasionally fight the dragons of my fears and to this day wonder whether I had the upper hand or ever will.

THE WORLD
IN THE MOLISHI

The Molishi was a small river, hardly a foot deep in dry season, twenty feet wide. It would not be on any map. Yet, in some improbable way, it once — for me — contained the world.

*

The independence of African countries led to guarded relations between peoples and races. Common interests and survival forced cooperation upon reluctant and suspicious partners. So when our mining company decided to supply each of our camps with a 12-bore shotgun, the weapon delivered to our camp was placed in the custody of the native camp boss whilst the ammo was put in my hands, as the still-expatriate mine manager. The weapon was the company's contribution towards self reliance in food supplies in those troubled times: our workers were encouraged to grow their own crops in the fields — shambas — reclaimed from the high forest and the shotgun was meant to keep pests away from the crops, primarily baboons and gorillas in these high hills of Africa.

Victor, an alert and yet discomfortingly quiet supervisor, was the appointed hunter. The hunting drill called for workers to alert him in case of intrusions in the shambas. Victor would then collect the shotgun from the camp boss and a sparse supply of cartridges from me: one cartridge for the kill, one to make up for a wounding shot and one to save his life if it all went wrong. Facing an angry adult gorilla with a shotgun is a daunting proposition, even when it's loaded with grape shots.

The local Bakumu tribe had deep roots in the forest and its members were partial to gorilla meat, probably on account of the virtues of power and manhood that eating it supposedly conferred. Be that as it may, Victor was underhandedly encouraged by our workers and the local population to focus on providing meat for them rather than protecting the banana plantations. So one particular morning, following the report of a sighting of a group of gorillas by a team of timber men, Victor silently disappeared into the forest with the shotgun and three cartridges. He emerged at about 3pm that afternoon reporting that he had killed an adult gorilla and a younger animal some five kilometers away towards the head of the Molishi river. He needed help to carry the carcasses.

*

Taking charge, I rallied eight keen hands and together we embarked in the battered Land-Rover pickup assigned to our tin mine. A bumpy dirt track followed the stream for a couple of kilometers. We drove to the farthest possible dropping point. There, being curious of the aftermath of the hunt, I locked up the vehicle and joined the trek. The path meandered through high forest, tall bushes and watercourses in low hills. As the sun set, we reached the two gorilla bodies which Victor had laid out at the foot of a tree. There was little blood. Victor had made efficient use of his cartridges with one to spare. The adult was a female of about 120 kilos, the youngster also a female of maybe half that size. In the fading light the men used their pangas to cut vines and sturdy young trees. In a few moments we had makeshift frames from which to hang the bodies. They also made torches with the sap of a local shrub, wrapped in large banana leaves. The night fell as we set off. The pungent smell of wild animals, of blood and death, and the prospect of a feast of meat triggered a joyous mood among the men like drunkenness. They began to sing. From his position at the head of the column of men, Victor did not join the merriment.

I walked between the two groups of porters. Because of the size of the loads, we hiked in the shallow waters of the Molishi rather than across the hills. The water felt cold through the rubber of my boots. There was a light breeze. From time to time I had a whiff of the gorillas' smell. The cooling atmosphere had undercurrents of warmer air. The kasuku torches threw erratic shadows on the black walls of trees on either side of the stream. When the strain of portering became too much, the songs slowly died away. The splashes at our feet were soon the dominant sounds in the night. The sky was bright with stars.

Not a soul outside our little world would know where we were. Nor would they care. We could disappear in the sands of the Molishi and there would not be a ripple on the face of the earth. Yet our primeval party had it all: death for some, the promise of life-giving food for others.

*

For two hours that night I was the brother of eight hungry Africans, of a silent killer and of two dead gorillas. Forty years later I still feel the cold of the water through those boots, and long for the peace of that evening to last forever.

35

The Rebel, the Dynamite and the Fish

"Michel! What the hell did you do? The rice is full of hair!"

Like any conscientious craftsman faced with a professional disaster for which he is not responsible, Michel Makanya, my friendly cook and factotum, assumed a pose of despondent frustration: "That is the way the Simbas cut up the goat, Bwana! They have no sense! I couldn't remove the skin from the ribs, and after cooking, the hair got into everything." Michel always did his best and there was no point harassing him for our plight. Our tin mine was cut off from all civilized supplies and we had to survive with what we had, including hairy rice. I tried to segregate edible food from the mess. After a while I gave up, pushed the plate aside and walked to the verandah of the bungalow. I could see the mine's cluster of administrative and support buildings, half a mile away at the end of the dirt road going down from the residential hill occupied by the senior staff. The corrugated roofs of the office, central store, carpentry and other workshops were visible in the green carpet of tall trees. Further below, I could make out the hospital, the labor camp and the football pitch where the executions had taken place.

Unable to pay the salaries, I began instead to distribute goods from the stores, demanding business as usual from our workers. Soon enough, the most desirable items—canned sardines, clothes and shoes—ran out and for the last pay-day there were only bags of paddy. The average worker was entitled to a carefully weighed gunny bag of un-decorticated rice each month. Congolese workers were not known for their thrift and most dedicated their income to the production of a foul alcohol. I could see the smoke from two or three dozen crude distilleries seeping through the canopy of the jungle. I had tried the product for want of a drink: the smell was vile, the taste repulsive and the effect near lethal. I shrugged my shoulders in helpless annoyance.

*

The Congo had been independent for three chaotic years. The first prime minister, Patrice Lumumba, was murdered after a very controversial term of six months in power. The country had been in constant turmoil, starting with the secession of the Katanga province, followed by the creation of the Kasai Empire and permanent unrest in the East. Pierre Mulele, a follower of Lumumba, had then fomented a personal rebellion against the weak Kinshasa regime, creating his own self-supporting popular militia.

The Mulelist rebels had conquered two thirds of the Congo in the space of one month. The jungle was throbbing with the memory of Lumumba, with unspoken fears of greater wars and improbable hopes of a better future. The ghost of Lumumba was said to have risen from Lake Tanganyika and to be proceeding towards Kinshasa to exact revenge from the corrupt politicians who had sold away the independence of the black people. The loyal warriors of Pierre Mulele, in an irresistible upsurge of popular power, had taken the country by storm and established the rule of the "Armée Populaire de Libération Nationale".

Our quiet mining outpost, home to half a dozen Belgian staff and about one thousand Congolese workers and employees, had to accommodate a billeted garrison of twenty Simbas as Mulelists liked to call themselves. Simba in Swahili means "lion". Simbas were brave for a reason: the swearing in of Mulelist warriors included the grant of invulnerability by the witch doctors attached to the APLN. The sorcerers — munganga in Swahili — would don medical attire, red crosses and stethoscopes or religious paraphernalia combined with monkey skins and amulets in a grotesque, sometimes funny, and often frightening display. They acted as priests, nurses, magicians and political officers. The consecrated warrior had the power to turn flying bullets into water by shouting "Mai!" at the appropriate time. Better still, he could shout "Mulele mai", at larger caliber fire. The magic would be wasted if the Simba misbehaved, had sex, touched a non-consecrated human, stole, lied or disobeyed. The benefit of this rule to us, reluctant white guests of the Revolution, was that stealing from us also caused the protection to fail. However, if a Simba could persuade someone to part with the object of his desires, whatever the manner used, it wasn't considered a theft. Needless to say, acclaimed African ingenuity had developed countless means of persuasion to rob us of our most useful possessions like cars, radios, watches etc. The Simba would simply ask for a donation, sometimes making the effort of building up a story. More sophisticated officers or mungangas would claim a requisition for the benefit of the Armée Populaire, and even give a receipt for whatever loot had triggered their lust. Deprived of all supplies, the work of the mine came to a near standstill and our days were spent in tense idleness.

The rebel occupation had already lasted two months, during which we were cut off from the real world except for some crackling news broadcasts received on unreliable shortwave radios. Food became scarce. The relationship between mine personnel and the garrison troops had been through ups and downs. Upon arrival in the mine, the first group of Simbas, heedless of the magic protection, looted the safe and the warehouse. They raped and murdered a girl in the camp. Three of the Congolese executives of the mine were summarily executed. The cashier Michel Kalimashi and the store keeper Michel Ludju were killed to remove witnesses who could have reported the thefts to the senior echelon of the APLN. Gabriel, the supervisor of the carpentry, was the father of the unfortunate girl and I think they executed him for the same reason. The Mulelist killers forbad us to bury the bodies in order to make a lasting impression on our small community. Michel Kalimashi was shot with a single bullet in the abdomen. He died after an agony of 30 hours during which workers gave me a regular account of his pain. In fear of the Simbas, the workers themselves set up a picket of guards equipped with spears and pangas around Michel as he died, to prevent his family from helping him. To my long-lasting remorse, I didn't attempt to broker any kind of relief for Michel Kalimashi during his ordeal.

*

After several weeks, we developed a way to interact with the rebels now established permanently in the mine and an uneasy cohabitation prevailed.

Adjutant Clement, the garrison commander, was a pragmatic person. He assessed that the glory derived from executing a few foreigners would be short-lived and was anyway outweighed by the advantages of exploiting our resourcefulness, or whatever was left of it. Clement was therefore tolerant of our existence, in a remote manner, having given much of a free hand to his Simbas to use us and to his munganga witch doctors to abuse us with their requisitions and extortions. Yet we were surviving.

The lack of variety in our diet became a severe nuisance: boiled rice at breakfast wasn't our idea of comfort. Boiled rice three times a day was severe harassment. I had goat meat on occasions, badly butchered, hairy and chewy, courtesy of Clement. We also had the odd chicken to keep the pretence of variety. I was underfed and fed up at the same time. We were living in a permanent state of fear, with no prospect of relief. The occasional outings to Bukavu, the provincial capital, with its bars and girls, the coolness of Primus beer and the sound of African jazz had become dreams of a distant past. As for Belgium, it was better not to think about it. We were truly on our own.

In the days before the rebellion, we had started to dispose of the couple of tons of old leaking dynamite we had in the explosives store, left over from a long-gone era. Dynamite is a mixture of nitroglycerin—which by itself is highly unstable—and a special sand to stabilize it. With age, dynamite exudes the nitroglycerin and becomes dangerous to use. We would blow up a few cases every once in a while, attempting to make some use of it despite its deteriorating state by blasting boulders or removing large tree stumps. The disposal however was complicated by unreliable pyrotechnic fuses which had given us a few anxious moments.

Now, short of food but as resourceful as always, we figured we could use our remaining twenty crates of dynamite to catch some fish. Paul, our chief mechanic, and

Philippe Gaillard, the mine accountant, joined me in a delegation to Clement to request that he lend us back our van to reach the ponds. Clement was shocked to learn that we had dynamite in our possession at all and I could see the fear in his eyes as it dawned on him what potential danger his Simba garrison had been in. He immediately declared the dynamite requisitioned by the Armée Populaire de Libération Nationale and assigned a couple of troops to guard the explosives store.

This achieved, Clement listened carefully as we explained that, although the dynamite was unstable, we planned to use it to supplement our tedious diet with fish. He must have been bored with the food himself because he agreed to our plan with the condition that we operate under the supervision of an escort of crack Simba troops. A much-decorated witch doctor was assigned to command the expedition. His uniform was highly personalised. He wore a Baden-Powell hat emblazoned with a Red Cross badge, and sported patches of animal skin on his shoulders. His face was unshaven. His eyes were red from excessive smoking of the local cannabis. Overall, he had the agitated demeanor of a man in power but unsure of himself.

We piled into the van: Paul (who drove), Gaillard, Makanya, my cheerful cook-cum-houseboy Sylvain, the quarrying foreman, the witchdoctor, the six elite Mulelists and myself. The springs bent so much that the old van just about dragged itself along the ground, hitting it at every other pothole in the dirt road. Sitting in the back, my eyes fell on the two open crates of dynamite. To my horror I realized that whoever had collected the stuff from the explosives store had placed the unpredictable fuses on the unstable oily sticks of dynamite. I shouted to Paul to stop and hurriedly took the fuses to the front of the van. Not that it would make much difference in the event of a spontaneous explosion, but the whole thing was precarious enough without compounding the risk with another challenge to fate.

The pond in Makundju, twenty kilometres away from the mine central camp, was a man-made rectangular reservoir of some fifty by two hundred meters and maybe four meters deep. The water was a dirty bottle green and the visibility less than a couple of feet. Our noisy arrival had alerted the population of the Makundju mining outpost: children, old women and even a couple of shapely girls surrounded us, begging, teasing, stealing and laughing all at the same time. Some workers had abandoned their distilleries to join in the expected fun. The Simbas, however, commanded respect and a few shouts kept the crowd at bay. We gathered on the bank of the pond and Sylvain laid out our materials on the grass: the dynamite sticks, eight inches long, one inch in diameter, in their nitro-soaked greasy wrapper, the pencil-like fuses with one hollow end in which to insert the burning cord, the white Bickford. The crowd watched intently. Swimmers volunteered for fish collection and began speculating on the size of the harvest. One of the shapely girls winked at me and gave me a big smile.

Aware of the prestige at stake, I diligently prepared a bundle of four sticks of dynamite, inserted a fuse, and clamped a twelve-inch Bickford cord in the open end. In an elaborate and self-conscious ritual, I lit up an Albert Bleue and blew a large cloud of blue smoke. The spectators were all eyes. I applied the burning end of the cigarette to the cord. It sizzled with a spatter of sparks. I waited a couple of seconds to check that it was burning true. Then with what I thought was the ample gesture of a self-assured professional, I lobbed the package into the green murky water. There was a slight splash, somehow ludicrous in relation to the majesty of the moment. Then a few bubbles, then nothing.

A Bickford fuse cord burns at a rate of one yard in 90 seconds. One foot, 30 seconds. Thirty seconds is a hell of a long time. So we waited. And waited. And then we waited some more. I kept a discreet eye on my watch. One minute. Something was wrong. Damned fuses. I mumbled some irritated explanation for the benefit of the witch doctor. Paul and Gaillard knew what was going on and were chatting up the Simbas and the neighboring crowd to keep up appearances.

I had another bundle ready and, to compensate for other failing fuses, I inserted two of them of different lengths. I lit the longer cord followed by the shorter one with the stub of the Albert Bleue, and again lobbed the bundle into the water. Thirty seconds, forty-five, sixty, eighty. This was ridiculous. Now the munganga was mumbling irritably.

It wasn't the time for pussy-footing. I inserted no fewer than four fuses in the next bundle of dynamite sticks. The hanging cords looked like an overspill of spaghetti and I had some difficulty in igniting them in the sensible sequence of the longest first. After some nervous fumbling, my bomb was ready and I breathed a sigh of relief when it hit the water. Surely, it would blow. Surely.

It didn't blow. By now the munganga was becoming agitated. He ambled over from his troops to our group and back, gesticulating with his arms. The amulets hanging from his uniform produced a rattling sound which would have been amusing in other circumstances. He firmly declared that the Armée Populaire de Libération Nationale was paving the way forward, that neocolonialists were out, that laquais of imperialism were doomed and would be executed, and that I should abandon my clumsy efforts. He, the munganga, with his magical powers, would take over. That sounded bad. The dynamite was dangerous enough itself, and so was my munganga friend. What to do?

I feverishly offered to help him and, despite his state of self-intoxication, he saw that I could still be of some use. Relieved, I prepared yet another bundle of twelve dynamite sticks, inserted six fuses and lit them, creating what looked like some weird Christmas firework. I handed this to the witch doctor who fumbled with his hold on the explosives. I urged him to expedite and prepared to duck for cover. After an eternity of perhaps five seconds, the munganga threw the explosives, screaming "Mulele mai! Mulele mai!" Then he waited. We waited. Everyone was silent. Bubbles came to the surface to mark the spot. After a while, the bubbles slowed and disappeared. We had a problem. The APLN does not take sabotage kindly. Enemies of the people are sentenced, executed and judged, in that order and without hesitation or mercy.

I moved forward to anticipate his anger: "OK, OK, no need to get excited. We told you the problem with this old stuff. Just give us a chance. Look, I'm going to give you another pack. Look, these fuses are almost new!" Inside, however we were nervous. This idiot was on a short fuse and liable to blow up at any moment…

With practice, the munganga got his hold right on the next package. He screamed, "Hail Lumumba!" and the bundle of dynamite gracefully flew through the air with a tail of streaming white cords and red sparks. Plouf! This time I had used eight fuses and a prayer. Bubbles burst to the surface of the water. At that point the bottom of the pond must have been lined with explosives. We were mesmerized. And then a muted explosion lifted a circle of water, like a large inverted saucepan. A couple of silvery tilapia floated to the surface and with a cheer totally out of proportion to the size of the catch the swimmers jumped in the water to pick up the dead fish. One of the shapely girls came out of the water without fish but with her shirt clinging to her body: she could have won a wet T-shirt contest anywhere in the world.

But the munganga wanted our attention. "See! See!" he exulted. "When I shouted Mulele mai, the Simba magic prevented the explosion. When I invoked the name of our Leader, his magic ensured that the treason of the deceitful white man would not stand in the path of our glorious revolution!"

"Asshole!" I thought.

We continued to throw dynamite in the pond and achieved another couple of explosions. The yield was about one kilo of tilapia for ten kilos of explosives. Never mind. This clearly was another victory for the Armée Populaire de Libération Nationale. Even Clement seemed to think so.

I wish I had a picture of the wet T-shirt as a souvenir of the event. In the end we had one fish each: that is Paul, Gaillard, Clement, the munganga, Sylvain and myself. Michel Makanya, like Clement, thought it was a success.

THE FLIES

It had been a mistake to remove the doors of the Land-Rover. There was merit in being able to get out fast in case of an ambush, but now I had no protection against the afternoon sun and my bare legs were burning. I wasn't moving, but I could feel sweat trickling down my chest, soaking the shirt. The heat and humidity had removed any intention we may have had to step out of the vehicle, despite the stench.

I waved at the flies landing on my face and asked Louis again: "Don't you think we should bury them?"

He shrugged. "What for? We should be moving soon," he said.

As if to confirm his hope, the gunfire died in the distance.

Our vehicle was at the tail end of the convoy. Some two hundred or more motor vehicles—trucks, buses, jeeps and armored cars—were strewn on the dirt track in front of us, waiting for the mercenaries of the point company to clear the latest ambush. Our procession, now stranded, must have covered a couple of miles. There wasn't thing to do: just wait on this endless track, in this godforsaken, ghostly village for the fighting to turn our way, and wish that if some of us should get hurt, it would be the other guy.

Lifting an arm I wiped the sweat from my brow with the sleeve of my shirt, driving a few flies away. I didn't want to look again, but against my will my eyes came back to the bodies in the drain. The nearest, some ten feet away, was lying face down. The bullet had entered at the base of his skull and made the most damage at the exit, hidden from me. Still, I could see from the edge of the man's face, folded back, that it must have been blown open. It was resting against the dirt, in the manner of a book placed upside down by the reader. The hard-baked ground around it had absorbed only a little of the pool of blood, so the flies were having a feast. Someone had stolen the shoes. The trousers of the uniform were raised around the ankles. There was no belt, helmet or weapon. The next body had wounds in the belly, the guts spilled out. A large cloud of flies was hovering above the mess. He was the source of the smell.

Louis had sense on his side: digging in this ground wasn't a sensible proposition. And even if it was? This guy, given half a chance, would have shot us. Would he have buried me? Certainly not; eaten, maybe. Yet, I had now spent over an hour in his company. And shared his flies. His shape and the visible parts suggested a young soldier. I wondered at the pattern of his life, what joy he may have had, what accomplishments he would leave on our earth? His life had, in all likelihood, been fruitless, his body left to rot in a ditch.

What was the sense of this? why bother to have him born? A short, empty spell, snuffed away before it had a hint of meaning. He had probably attended a couple of years at a village school, where he would have repeated the asinine litanies of French spelling and learned the irrelevant history of Belgium. He probably had tended the shambas and kept the goats. The temptations of the city must have lured him to Kindu, most likely, where his choices had been to starve as a petty thief or to enlist in the army. A couple of months of inadequate training had made him no more than the pretence of a soldier, ill-equipped, badly prepared. What was his chance of survival in the gunsight of the mercenaries? His worthless life brought to a useless end, at the cost of a bullet.

I closed my eyes and tried to relax, ignoring the flies. Then a couple of them crawled across my face and picked at my lips. I chased them and looked at the bodies again. Did the guy have a mother? Sure he had one. Better if she never knew, though. That way she could still hope and dream. My mind drifted to my own situation. What if that bullet had hit my brains instead of his? Had my life a greater import than his? Had my achievements been more meaningful? Who was there to measure? Who cared?

A stir rippled down the line of vehicles. A couple of engines started. A few minutes later, we were on the move again. The speed, slow as it was, gave the impression of air. The flies stayed behind. The flies, and a weird, disturbing empathy.

THE EDGE
OF THE VOLCANO

Geography, climate and the Tanzanian National Parks Administration have joined forces to make the access to the top of Kilimanjaro a monumental staircase with four logical and roughly equal steps. The first step takes the unwary trekker from Mangaru Gate, at 1,900m, through picturesque rain forest to Mandara, at 2,700m. Streams and waterfalls worthy of Hollywood, tall trees, mossy vines, and watchful colobus monkeys entertain visitors as they easily stroll along. However, to put this in perspective, this stage of the ascent is already higher than most skiing resorts.

The second stage from Mandara to Horombo (3,720m) is equally pleasant. The start of the trail is reminiscent of the Isola Garden in London's Richmond Park. Exotic trees line the well-groomed path. This takes the still unsuspecting tourist through thinning vegetation to a height equal or above the spectacular Pic du Midi in Chamonix, Japan's Mount Fuji or the daunting Eiger in Switzerland. The trek is over relatively gentle slopes rounding off ridge after ridge. The journey is about 11km and still quite manageable. At

Horombo, you will be above the quasi-permanent layer of clouds of the dry season and the sun will be brighter than in Dubai.

Step three is from Horombo to Kibo Hut at 4,750m. This is nearly the height of Mont Blanc (4,807m), the highest mountain in the Alps. By now, the vegetation has gradually disappeared and the landscape is a rocky featureless desert, sloping between the growing mass of Kilimanjaro and the Mawenzi crater to the east. On a sunny day you will see Tanzania behind you and in front you will have glimpses of Kenya, including Mount Kenya. The wind even at midday has a distinct chill. You're at last looking the mountain in the eyes and the enormity of step four is overwhelming. Ancient volcanic eruptions and erosion have accumulated boulders and pebbles around the crater, forming a forbidding cone of loose materials around the base. The gravelly ground rests at the angle of natural repose for lose materials, between 35 and 40 degrees.

However the sight from Kibo Hut makes the gigantic hulk appear near vertical. At this point most tourists wonder whether this is really a good idea. The scree slope from Kibo takes you straight up to the edge of the crater at Gilman's Point (5,681m) and walking round the circumference of the crater will take you to Uhuru Peak, at 5,895m the official summit of Kilimanjaro, Africa's highest mountain and, incidentally, the highest free-standing mountain in the world.

I had figured that getting there was a matter of determination, gear, accessories, training and organization. As determination goes, mine was based on some lingering romanticism associated with earlier visits to Africa. There was also a vain desire to prove that having recently celebrated another significant birthday wasn't really the end of anything. Gear was easier. Being a seasoned traveler, having spent four years mining tin ore in the high hills of Eastern Congo and owning a holiday place in Haute-Savoie, I figured I had a sound understanding of Africa and of mountains. So I quickly packed a few Versace tee-shirts, jeans, some indifferent underwear, a thick jumper, old comfortable hiking boots and started off with a blissful forgetfulness of realities.

Accessories were equally simple: I had grabbed a toothbrush, a torchlight and some mosquito repellent, only to bitterly regret a few days later the lack of soap and hygiene paraphernalia, the absence of a comb, the paucity of drinking water, and above all having left behind all form of sun protection.

I had done marginally better at training and taken regular extended or fast walks, made some attempts at scaling heights such as Jebel Hafeet, and done a lot of stair-climbing, to 600 meters vertically on one occasion. To be truthful, the latter effort had left me with extremely sore legs and a slightly shaken — but not stirred — faith in my abilities.

My guardian angel however took care of the essentials in terms of organization. To begin with, the Marangu Hotel graciously provided additional clothing which, if somewhat surprising in color combinations, proved to be extremely useful. My appearance in these borrowed clothes caused Andy, a fellow climber, to laugh to tears for a solid ten-minute period.

Just as effectively, the Marangu Hotel provided forty-two porters and nine guides for our team of twenty-four. The unflinching endurance, thorough competence and attentive dedication of the African personnel cannot be praised enough.

Lastly, I must mention Diamox: this is a drug commonly prescribed to heart patients. One of its side effects is to minimize the symptoms of altitude sickness, usually felt as nausea, diarrhea, fever, shortness of breath and other drawbacks. A side effect of Diamox, however, is to make the patient urinate frequently. This aspect turned out to be a significant—if unexpected—preoccupation for most of us during the trip and particularly during the nights.

The rest of course should have been easy with intelligent strategic planning, like which pair of socks to keep for tomorrow, what water to carry, in which pocket to keep the lipstick and what to do with the litter.

That is where reality caught up.

The walk to Mandara was easy enough, despite the vague anticipation of the enormous mass looming beyond. After the evening meal was skillfully prepared and served by the Marangu Hotel gang, we settled in the sleeping huts. These were structures of triangular section, sleeping four people in a space of twelve by twelve feet. Here came another dimension of strategic planning. The night was cold and silent. The cold bit and the silence was awesome. The muted sounds of a sleeping bag zipper or the ruffle of nylon brushing nylon took on cataclysmic proportions. Visiting the loo for the frequent Diamox mission went like this: feeling for the torch and checking the time (to judge whether to hang on or not), unzipping the sleeping bag, fumbling for glasses, groping for trousers and pulling them on, pulling on a thick top, putting boots on and swearing silently at uncooperative laces, quietly opening the door, all the while filtering the torch light with your fingers and minimizing commotion.

Finally emerging from the sleeping hut was a relief also because of the fresh air and the unique feel of the African night. That night I had a first taste of what altitude does to people. I woke up with a wildly racing heart, gulping hopelessly for air. No matter how fast I attempted to breathe, my heart was racing away. That and an awful sense that I was trapped in the cubicle. Wild options flew through my distraught mind: walking back down through the night, getting out and standing outside, each proposition as impractical as the other. The sense of losing it and the helplessness were terrifying. Then my guardian angel woke up, the panic slowly subsided and a blissful sleep came back. I will never chain an animal again.

The next day took us to Horombo, an easy enough walk. We stayed two nights at the Horombo huts, with an idle day for acclimatization. The two nights at Horombo however extended the discomfort, highlighting the inadequacies of my personal arrangements. I began to suffer small nose bleeds and couldn't figure out if they were related to altitude. Just in case, I increased my intake of Diamox. After the first night at Horombo, Jose left us without taking the acclimatization day. He was a friendly soft-spoken Colombian who had joined us at Marangu. He was an adventure freak who would run twenty miles in the morning, mountain bike fifty in the afternoon and canoe the night away, upstream I have no doubt.

Setting off for the dormant volcanic cone of Kibo after the second night in Horombo came as a relief. I managed a good pace, reaching Kibo in four hours or so against the Park assessment of five. In the end however, as the slope was steeper towards the foot of the crater cone, I sensed tiredness and stiffness in the thighs and hips. On the way, I saw Jose coming down from his climb to the summit in the early morning. He was cheerful as usual and imparted his advice. "Go real slow", he said. "I left Kibo at one o'clock this morning, got to Uhuru at five and had to sit in the dark for one hour to see the sun rise. Take it easy."

"Oh really? Thanks, Jose." I already knew I would not rush it. "Have no fear, Jose."

We arrived at Kibo at about two pm and had tea. The wind there had a nasty bite. The huts, made of stones, were drafty and unwelcoming. I performed the usual strategic planning (this in that pocket and that in this pocket), had dinner at five thirty and was in bed by six pm.

The plan was to get up at eleven thirty the same evening, get our gear and clothing in order and set out on the last leg by one am or earlier. By then the discomfort had taken its toll and most of us felt filthy and unshaven. I should have had a crew-cut. It is said that the guides get their customers on their way in the middle of the night because any sane adult would turn down the idea in day time, so forbidding was the appearance of the scree.

Charles, the chief guide, led the way, taking it real slow to preserve our breath and energy for the awesome effort ahead. In the night, the climbers were black silhouettes in a long single line against the whitish background of the mountain. The moon was at three quarters and soon cast enough light for most of us to switch off our torches. The scene was ghostly as very few of us still had breath to talk.

After half an hour we had a first stop to drink. The pause was clearly welcome to most. Then the slow motion resumed with great effort. The next pause was even more welcome and from then on the party broke up into small groups. I found myself in the last of these, having judged my pace insufficient to keep up with Charles and the other leaders.

From that point, the going got even slower, most climbers stopping for breath after every twenty steps or so. The word "step" here must be understood in context: a step was a forward movement of one foot of about eight to twelve inches. Sometimes it was aborted because the gravel rolled under the sole of the boot. Sometimes it was shaky. Sometimes it was zero inches. The climbers were rocking sideways a little bit, like dancing bears, and their sideways movement appeared more pronounced than the forward one.

To keep my mind busy and distracted from the pains of the hours ahead, I counted my steps. Then I tried to add them up. Before long I realized that simple arithmetic was eluding me completely. I struggled for a while with thirty-five plus seventeen, made it thirty-five, then realized it was wrong but was unable, between fast breathing and slow thinking, to come up with the right answer.

After each of these pathetic forward dashes we rested till the breathing calmed down, standing and slowly vacillating. Upon the start of every new "dash" I stumbled badly, like a drunken man leaving the safety of his bar rail. Initially I thought this was an effect of the steep, uneven path and of my half-dead right foot (a paragliding mishap a few years before). Then I noticed bright spots on the trail and couldn't figure whether these were pebbles reflecting the moon or something else. After a while I had to acknowledge that hypoxia—shortage of oxygen—was taking its toll. The symptoms were the gradual loss of mental functions, loss of balance, and hallucinations.

The going deteriorated from bad to worse. Still far from Gilman's Point, I decided that I would turn back as soon as I reached the edge of the crater and I would not attempt to climb Uhuru Peak. I felt it unwise to push further as it might cause me to become a danger to myself and a nuisance to my companions. I also knew that the descent would use different muscles in my legs and the exercise might rapidly become stressful.

The sun came up at six thirty and I reached Gilman's Point on the crater at about seven am. It had taken six hours to cover a distance of about three kilometers and gain an altitude of nine hundred and fifty meters. I took a few photos, had a cup of tea courtesy of a porter carrying a flask, and started the descent.

It was as painful as I had anticipated. I reached the Kibo Hut at nine am, and continued on to Horombo in the afternoon sunshine. Another night at Horombo added to the uncleanliness misery but allowed for a solid twelve hours sleep without Diamox interruptions. The last day took us to Marangu by way of Mandara. Cool drinks and hot baths were at long last available.

At Kibo on the morning of the climb, I saw the other climbers stumbling into the hut after their trek to Uhuru. I do not recall a single one smiling. Everybody was utterly drained and fully focused on finding a bunk.

The private elation came a day or two later and with it realization that the Kilimanjaro trek was primarily a journey within oneself: an acid test in an exotic setting. Some climbers find meaning in their achievement; others wonder why they went so far to find something which was with them all along.

This was how I felt. As a holiday, scaling Kilimanjaro was far too stressful and uncomfortable. The views were great but not great enough, even when I was in good enough shape to formulate a judgement.

I amuse myself by suggesting that the trek may be suitable for honeymooners, as a good friend once observed about such remote locations. All it takes is to find a way to do it in absolute silence.

At the Marangu Hotel I bought a tee shirt with the slogan: "Kilimanjaro—Too High To Explain" and went back to work.

ARABIA

HAMDAN

THE GHOST HORSE

In those near biblical years the area past the race course at Malaz was a large flat desert stretching a couple of miles eastward to the low hills of Kashm El Han and eight to ten miles south between the farm of Prince Mohammed bin Saud Al Kebir and the Yamamah cement works. Most stables were located near the race track and the compact ground of the plain offered good wandering opportunities to riders.

Hamdan, my chestnut stallion, was short and stocky. He had a prancing pace, a lion's heart, an irrepressible urge to gallop, and poor eyesight. Being a fairly green rider at the time and finding it hard to induce other mounts into a good canter, I bought Hamdan for his unrestrained dash and uncomplicated behavior. Our relationship settled into one defined by his runaway vigor and my cautious disposition, the prudence of the neophyte still tainting my equestrian eagerness. I rode Hamdan with a full bridle, though whenever we competed in local gymkhana events, this could make jumping hazardous. My clumsy hands often interfered with Hamdan's enthusiasm and caused many spectacular crashes through oxers and other jumping obstacles. I must say to Hamdan's credit that even though we scored countless faults on account of knockdowns, we never had refusals. Hamdan was a brave horse.

This particular Friday we left in the cool early hours of the morning. Skirting the hills, we made a long clockwise oval trek and by ten o'clock we had Prince Mohammed's farm in sight and the prospect of a well-deserved lazy day ahead of us. Our indolent pace was suddenly checked, however, by the unusual feature of a ditch that cut across the desert, perpendicularly to our intended path back home. The ditch was about seven feet deep and four feet wide. A shallow heap of spoil materials ran along the opposite side.

Slightly perplexed, I explored the options. To the right: no end to the cursed obstacle in sight. Left: the same. Front: the tempting farm in the distance, the heap of spoils on the opposite edge, the breadth of the trench. Down: the depth of the trench. I looked again, hoping our prospects might have changed, but found the same endlessness, the same breadth, the same depth. Obviously if we backtracked we could make it home without complication in a couple of hours. The prospect however wasn't attractive after an already long trek and a growing thirst. And after all, I was a rider and Hamdan was a jumping horse. So what was holding me?

The decision was one thing but execution was another. It wasn't that the trench was that wide. But it was deep. Hamdan and I had a number of heavy crashes behind us, with a broken tooth and a torn shoulder ligament to stir my prudence. I dismounted and, holding the reins, gracefully leaped across the obstacle. That achieved, I stood on the opposite edge and proceeded to induce Hamdan to follow. I tugged at the reins to show him the way. Hamdan shook his head and shied from the rim. Our dance lasted a while with little progress either way, and we remained precariously balanced on our respective edges of the ditch. Then Hamdan could resist his own courageous nature no longer and he jumped towards me.

For a split second I congratulated myself for the beauty and solidity of my plan. But almost at once, the brink of the ditch crumbled under the impact of Hamdan's landing hind hooves. The stallion scrambled wildly with his hind quarters but gravity took over and Hamdan fell. Gaining his feet, he found himself standing on the bottom of the ditch, pointing west and unable to turn in the narrow channel. I still had the reins in my hand.

It is not the done thing for a rider to appear back at the stables on foot. Besides, they were still some distance away and what would happen to Hamdan? My only option was west, in the direction Hamdan was pointing, and I started walking, tugging at the reins to get the horse to follow me. I quickly found that the reins were a little too short for the vertical distance separating my hand from Hamdan's mouth and he was clearly uncomfortable with his head twisted upwards. Deciding I could just as well be in the ditch myself, I jumped down and led him from the front. Hamdan was now more comfortable but my going was tiring as the excavator had loosened the bottom of the trench and walking on soft sand was hard work. Also, my face was below the edge of the ditch. A light wind skimmed the surface of the desert and blew sand in my eyes. Between the sensations of growing thirst, sore feet and runny eyes, the thought re-occurred to me that Hamdan was still a horse and I a rider.

Worming my way between the wall of the ditch and Hamdan's flank I managed to get back in the saddle. This provided immediate bliss for my feet and my eyesight quickly cleared. There was still no end to the cursed ditch in sight, though. My shoulders were now just above ground level and I had a limited view of the surroundings. I spotted a Bedouin encampment next to the ditch about two hundred meters ahead. Half a dozen Bedouins were squatting on the sand brewing tea, in plain intimate vista of my inescapable route.

Despite my annoyance and distress, it was clearly a time for composure. I straightened myself, and lifted my shoulders an inch or so above the desert flatness. At the distance dictated by the most refined protocol I uttered a clear "Salam aleikum" with the straight face and natural demeanor of the practiced orientalist, my confidence making it clear that I was in my natural environment. Not to be undone the Bedouins replied "Assalam aleikum" with an equally straight face and friendly courtesy. These were people of the desert, familiar with stories of spirits and apparitions, unsurprised to find me riding a ghost under the shifting sands.

The Taking of VW3

In those blessed years in Saudi Arabia, as an English friend observed, no foreigners had spoiled our country yet. A case of smuggled Johnnie Walker was available for 300 Saudi rials—about eighty dollars. We were merrily blasting deep trenches through Riyadh's rocky underground to build a sewerage network and the extensive use of explosives in the heart of an already crowded city was still considered acceptable. Saudi justice was regularly enforced through spectacular public displays of lashing and beheading after the Friday prayers. The less frequent mutilation of confirmed thieves had, however, become a somewhat surgical affair, with doctors in attendance rather than swordsmen, but the threat of amputation was still very present and the country was the safest on earth.

When it came to the safekeeping of property, therefore, trust bordered on carelessness. It was common to leave cars unlocked with their windows open and the keys in the ignition. So that particular morning, after making my tour of the company working sites and returning by eight am to our mess hall, a villa in Malaz suburb, I left the Beetle, company number 3, in front of the gate, with its windows wound down and the key in the ignition.

Breakfast was always a welcome interruption at the start of the day, but our busy schedules seldom allowed time for loitering in the dining room. That morning, I was out in a few minutes. The Beetle had disappeared! Annoyed more than angry, I enquired with colleagues whether one of them had borrowed the car or if the workshop had picked it up for some unscheduled service. No, the car had evaporated. Double check: same result. The conclusion became obvious. So much for chopping off hands: amputation clearly didn't deter everybody!

Back in the office, I faced reality. Our secretary and administrative factotum, Mamdouh, prepared an elaborate plea in flowery language to the Malaz police station to report the theft of VW3. I signed the lengthy petition and, whilst Mamdouh proceeded to the police station, I borrowed another car from our small pool to go back into town.

The second car turned out to be a Chevy II, an American compact in the fashion popular at the time. It was the epitome of the donkey car—a very old and tired donkey. Nevertheless it took me down Passport Road at a reasonable pace. There I suddenly noticed VW3 cruising leisurely past to my right. Positive ID was no problem since our cars sported their company serial numbers on the front doors in the most unmistakable manner.

The driver of the Beetle was in the native garb: dishdash, gutrah and headgear. He was engaged in an animated conversation with a companion in similar attire. Their windows were down to enjoy the still-cool morning air.

VW3 was our property and I wanted it back, so I drove abreast of the errant vehicle and hit the horn, waving with my right hand to indicate that the driver should pull to the right and stop. The man was visibly startled. When he looked at me he seemed to realize that his joy ride had turned sour.

For a split second, the thief held his course. Likewise, I held mine and we went on in a suspended eternity of our own. Then he hit the throttle and, to the eternal credit of our mechanics, VW3 leapt forward and cut across my path.

This was serious stuff! I had recently seen Steve McQueen giving chase to baddies in the streets of San Francisco in the movie *Bullitt*. My sense of righteousness and confidence were fueled with adrenaline.

I appraised my resources: a tank three quarters full, a riding whip on the back seat and my six-foot frame against a couple of shorter guys. The chase was on and I would not let go as long as I could coerce my Chevy donkey into a reasonable gallop.

The VW swerved in front of me in heavy traffic and hit the back of a dumper truck. The crash caused a small dust cloud, and the amateur thief wove about more to regain control. By now we were in front of the Passport Office and there was a large crowd of PROs (public relations officers — the consecrated way to refer to errand clerks) milling about. The driver had more trucks and other traffic to the front and a hot pursuer behind. I wasn't letting go of the horn. His only way forward was through the crowd on the broad sidewalk to our right.

The PROs leaped right and left to get out of the way of the maverick vehicle. Their thobes were flying. Their flight was reminiscent of seagulls taking off from a beach. It was a miracle that nobody got hurt. Undeterred, my opponent moved on through thinning traffic. If this helped him, it helped me too and I got very close to his tail. I had already assessed that the chase could go on for another two hours before the thief could shake me loose. Whatever mayhem would ensue wasn't my responsibility but theirs and I rejoiced in the thought.

My determination must have showed because I squeezed my way through the traffic again until I was level with the hijackers of our property.

I saw frantic exchanges between the driver and his companion. They were clearly agitated and, despite the sluggish response of the Chevy, I edged forward and pushed them to the right kerb. As we stopped in a screech of tires and a wail of my horn, the sudden silence was deafening and I could see the thieves shivering.

The Beetle looked battered. The front showed an imprint of the truck's backside and the right door had been scraped by the Passport Office front wall. By chance, our chase had ended in front of an official building on the incline leading to the Nassriyeh Palace. I summoned the sentry on guard in broken Arabic. Through a combination of gestures, a display of licenses, ID, business card and VW registration papers—extracted from the Beetle glove compartment under the nose of the bemused thief—I developed some kind of understanding with the soldier. His fellow sentries had now joined in and I managed to get the whole lot of them—thief included—into the VW and the Chevy. We drove in convoy back to the Malaz police station.

As we reached the Station, we saw Mamdouh coming out of the building, having registered our claim for the stolen Beetle. The commander of the station was immediately appreciative: this was turning out to be the fastest case of his career, the claim and the culprit being delivered at the same time. He assured us most courteously that the thief would have his right hand removed. In the meantime, he ordered his policemen to shackle the thief in an old-fashioned assembly of timber frame, steel manacles, chains and padlocks. Off we went, Mamdoueh and I.

Late that evening my friend Harb, an astute Saudi facilitator and now a very rich man, called to request a favor. One of his close friends wanted to see me as a matter of urgency. I couldn't deny him this small courtesy and we agreed that the friend would see me at 7.30 the next morning in our office.

Rather intrigued, I waited for the visitor and at 7.30 exactly in walked a police general in full regalia—medals, fourragère, headgear, riding crop and so on. He introduced himself hurriedly and went on to explain that he was a very unfortunate person: his son was ill, the mother was severely distressed, the household was in disarray and his meager stipend as a general hardly covered the doctors and pharmacy bills.

I expressed polite sympathy for the general's ordeal and enquired about the point of the visit. "Well, ahem," he replied, "my son's illness really is mental and manifests itself in irrational behavior."

The son's most recent fit, apparently, caused him to borrow, most irresponsibly, the motorcar of our company.

The general went on to promise that he would foot the bill for the repairs to the Beetle. Further, he wondered if we would be kind enough to withdraw our claim at the Malaz police station so that a poor mother's grief should not be compounded further.

THE MAUVE GHOST (A LIBYAN TALE)

"Mouammou! Did you pack your slippers?"

Exasperated, Aisha threw out of the suitcase a gold-plated Kalashnikov AK47 and several magazines of ammunition. She removed a crystal picture frame displaying a signed photograph of her husband standing with President Sarkozy.

"No way will I have a picture of this jerk in my house for the rest of my life!" she said as she threw the offending image away.

She rummaged further in the Louis Vuitton trunk and got rid of an assortment of gaily-colored dildos. Twelve leather-bound copies of the Green Book soon landed on the heap of discarded items, together with a couple of heavily-embroidered uniforms stacked with medals. They could hear muted gunfire through the bullet-proof glazing. There were palls of black smoke drifting across the skyline of Tripoli.

Colonel Qaddafi, his face a grimace of repressed irritation, picked up a rosy dildo with one hand and a Green

Book with the other. He faced the formidable figure of his wife.

"I will not leave without essential supplies," he declared, brandishing what he considered his essentials. He walked back to the suitcase to re-pack his traveling kit. "My mission is not over. The Libyan people will come to their senses. Give them a month! No, not a month, one week! They will beg me to lead the revolution again!"

"Ok, Mouammou. But in the meantime, we have to get out of here. We have to move. And no heavy suitcases! Saif has arranged a Corolla for us. It's a small car, you know." She removed the dildo and the Green Book again and closed the trunk with a thump.

"What? A Corolla? I want the silver-lined Maybach! Is Saif out of his mind? Who does he think we are?"

The concussion of a rocket explosion caused the window frame to rattle.

"Shut up, Mouammou! Take your clothes off and put this on. We have no time now. Hurry up." Aisha had a gown folded on her forearm. She went to her husband and proceeded to open the collar of his battledress. "You should stop pretending, you know. You're too old for this, Mouammou. The last time you fired a gun, you missed a duck at three feet!" She pulled his arms out of the sleeves, threw the coat on the pile of rejects and opened the buckle of his belt.

Holding his belt-less trousers with two hands over his paunch, the colonel protested: "I told Saif no way would I run away dressed as a woman!"

Another explosion, louder this time, shook the window.

Undeterred, Aisha took his hands away, slapped them as if he were a child and pulled his trousers down. Muammar stood in a mauve singlet and boxer shorts with green and white stripes, his warrior's garments now scattered on the floor. He stepped back, ready to fight off the lady-like bedecking.

"Your choice, Mouammou. I'm fed up with your antics. Do you want to die here? Not unless you sign me onto the Swiss bank accounts. I have not put up with forty years of living with you to lose everything now. Get dressed!"

As if punctuating Aisha's admonition, several shots echoed in the room, much closer now. It sounded like the battle had moved into some parts of the palace. Aisha grabbed the gown still on her arm and rolled it up so as to pass the garment over Muammar's head. The colonel stepped backward till he felt the door handle pressing against his buttocks. With the support of the Libyan nation, he had been able to face Aisha, somehow. Now he was alone. Terribly alone.

In frenzy, he turned around, opened the door, and ran out, his colorful silhouette fading as it got farther and farther towards the desert.

He has not been seen since.

74

THE CATCH

The chairman had a hooked nose, a thin black moustache and dark regular features under the white gutrah. The chairman was polished, cultured, smooth in appearance and courteous in manners. His simmering anger could only be seen in the staccato tapping of his golden pen against the edge of the conference table. John, the finance director of the consortium, had just reported an anticipated loss of 107 million dollars for the year. The chairman turned towards the CEO of the construction management company.

"Tell me again, will you. I want to understand how this five-billion-dollar project has been brought to a standstill by a crummy outfit mistakenly entrusted with a paltry ten-million-dollar sub-contract." The bullying and bragging wasn't the chairman's style. It revealed his frustration. He slammed the pen on the table and the assembled directors mentally stood to attention.

Dave Houston, the management company CEO, was an articulate operator. The dark pinstripe suit, the silk shirt and the Hermes tie highlighted a healthy tan acquired on exclusive ski slopes and expensive beach resorts. He was a man of the world, experienced and secure in his understanding of developers, contractors and construction generally. He cleared his throat and started: "Mr Chairman, may I remind the Board that Houston Projects, as manager of your estate development, expressed reservations about awarding the reclamation contract to Dredgers Incorporated. Their track record involves only small projects, none of which comes near the size of our requirement; their equipment has not been inspected and their management is amateurish. Only the price was attractive. This is what you get when you go for the cheapest tender."

The chairman's anger rose for all to see: "Mr Houston, we shall debate responsibilities in due course. Pray tell us the options at hand right now to satisfy the shareholders, pacify the banks and control the buyers."

Dave Houston self-consciously adjusted his platinum cufflinks. "The bottom line is this, Mr Chairman: Dredgers had to bring a shallow draft cutter dredger from the Far East. In the first place the vessel sailed three months late. Then she got impounded in Colombo during a stopover on account of unsettled fuel bills and an ancient feud between Dredgers and the Sri Lankan Port Authority.

"All this is hearsay of course.

"There is no relief in sight for the time being. We could cancel the Dredgers contract and tender the land reclamation package again. We have identified only two suitable dredging companies with the right type of equipment: one is in Alaska and is starting a two-year contract with Mobil Oil; the other is in the Caspian Sea. The unit in the Caspian Sea may be released in about six months. At that point it would have to sail up the Volga, through the canal link to the Don river and down to the Black Sea. The sailing time to the Persian Gulf would be around a month and a half. With this latter option, the reclamation could be executed with an overall delay of thirteen months on our initial schedule. In the meantime we could seize the Dredgers performance bond—worth one million, two hundred thousand dollars—which you hold in the form of an irrevocable bank guarantee, payable on demand."

"Bravo!" cried the chairman. Uncharacteristically sarcastic, he continued: "And how do you propose to apportion the one million, two hundred thousand dollars, Mr Houston? A five-thousand dollar rebate to each of the buyers of our apartments to keep them quiet whilst they wait? A half-million dollar fee to prevent the banking syndicate foreclosing on our repayment schedule? And perhaps a special dividend of five dollars to each of our ten thousand shareholders? In the meantime we incur a direct operational loss of 107 millions, not to mention the loss of profit!"

The chairman's harangue had been also atypically long. He concluded by addressing the finance director: "John, do you have the Dredgers Incorporated contracts?"

John shuffled through the folder in front of him, picked up a paper and walked around the table to hand it to the chairman. The chairman glanced through the document, stood up and walked alone to his adjacent office. He closed the door behind him. The directors looked at each other, remaining silent. Dave Houston was looking out the window at the Dubai Business Bay. Despite the silky air-conditioned environment, the atmosphere in the conference room was oppressive.

*

In The Hague, Jan De Sterke, the all-in-one owner, managing director, chief engineer and ops manager of Dredgers Incorporated was having an early coffee with the captain of his new suction dredger. The phone was buried under a heap of open drawings and Jan had to dig deep to grab the receiver. "Jan De Sterke speaking. Good morning." He listened for a long while and then continued. "Mr Chairman, Dredgers sincerely regrets this situation. However, yes, an extra five million dollars on the contract will enable Dredgers to release the vessel from Colombo. Still, I must request — and have your agreement — that our performance bond will be returned forthwith, as Dredgers can no longer be exposed to either penalties or the contract termination clauses. Likewise, payment has to be from an escrow account in The Hague, through pre-released demand drafts. On the other hand, yes, I give you my word that the dredger will be in the Gulf in two weeks and that your project will be completed in three months."

Jan listened intently for another long spell. "Yes, Mr Chairman, we have a deal. I will fax you the details of our bank account for the five-million-dollar advance on the contract and I will work on Colombo right away. Thanks for your understanding and support. My respects, Mr Chairman."

*

Back in the conference room, the chairman was looking at Dave Houston. "Mr Houston, you will see fit to send me a letter requesting the cancellation of the contract of Houston Projects with our development consortium. You will also see fit, I hope, to waive your fee for the last six months. On receipt of your letter I will confirm that we have no claims against your firm. John here will do the paperwork. In the meantime, John, come with me into my office. I have some pressing instructions for you."

Dave Houston suddenly appeared pale under his tan. Somehow, the silk shirt and the Hermes tie had lost their lustre.

*

Meanwhile in The Hague, Jan De Sterke was on the phone again. "Hi, Bala, old chap! How is Colombo? Hot? Lucky you! We are freezing our balls off here!" He paused for a while to listen to his correspondent. "Yes, it worked a treat. I will have a hundred thousand dollars wired to your Geneva account as soon as I get the transfer from the Gulf. Same number as last time, yes? I will call you immediately it's done, so that you can officially send our vessel on its way. And next time your Ministry needs expert dredging, please think of us again. We enjoyed working in Ceylon before and we will again, I'm sure!" Jan put the phone down with a smile.

MISSED

It had been over ten minutes since the black Land-Rover had passed me, but my hands seemed to be shaking more and more, with a willful life of their own. Lighting a cigarette took three attempts and I let it drop twice to the floor. I had parked the Chevrolet on the road shoulder and sat on the bonnet as I didn't trust my legs to stand up. There was hardly any traffic and birds were chirping in the nearby thorn trees. The light desert breeze of the morning was caressing my face, giving an illogical, barely tolerable background of peacefulness to my agitated state.

*

The nearness of violent death does not trigger a flash memory; it presents no fast forward review of one's prominent life events. However the brutal rush of adrenaline creates an extraordinarily heightened perception. Details acquire the crispness of an *eau-forte*, an etching; smells are suddenly noticed, noises recorded in detail.

And so is imprinted in my head the sight of the driver of the Land-Rover: the expressionless aquiline face of a Bedouin, his dark eyes and brows under the white gutrah, the short black beard, the square shape of the rushing vehicle, the dull green of the Mercedes tipper truck. Twenty years on and the swooshing scream of the onrushing vehicles still pierces my ears and my memory.

*

It was just another day at the office. I left Dubai early for a meeting in Al Ain. Dubai wasn't yet on the map and the dual carriageway was still an empty country road that produced a gentle rollercoaster motion over low dunes. The police were friendly in manner and unsophisticated in operation. Speeding wasn't quite a sin and I wasn't used to a slow pace. I must have been cruising at just over 100mph. There was no traffic. The road was leading up a small hillock and I was approaching the top when a truck appeared, coming in the opposite direction on the lane to my left. The six-wheeler tipper was fully loaded and moving steadily, a rock-solid mass of 50 tons. And right in front of me was the black Land-Rover, overtaking the truck at high speed. Our combined approach speed must have exceeded 200mph.

Death was staring at me with blazing eyes. In a fraction of a fraction of a second, I decided to take evasive action towards the hard shoulder on the right side of the road. If the momentum of the Chevrolet caused me to overshoot, the desert was reasonably flat, a couple of feet below the banking edge of the hard shoulder.

The average human brain takes about a fifth of a second to translate a thought into muscular impulse. My arm was already cocked to pull the driving wheel when the Land-Rover drifted to the right and on to the hard shoulder. In a blink, the three vehicles were in a line abreast: the tipper truck to the left, my Chevrolet in the middle and the black station wagon trailing a plume of dust on the hard shoulder.

Then the other two were gone. I had not moved.

For a few seconds, everything was in suspension: the humming of the engine, the steady feel of the wheel, the sound of the air rushing along the body of the car. Then my heart beat increased. I had missed the death train by a mere fifth of a second. And yet nothing was changed: the Chevrolet didn't have a scratch and my hair was unruffled. A miss, no matter how close, is as if the event never existed; there were no physical consequences. But still the shadows of what could have been would darken my life. How many times could one miss the death train?

I stopped and my hands started shaking.

TRIPLE-CROSS

1. At the Polo Club

Jon

Dubai, 4pm. The working day was drawing to a close. Even in winter, the afternoon sun was warm but it was coming down now. In the shadows of the buildings, the air had a touch of coolness. Traffic had started to build up.

I got in the car, pulled the roof down and enjoyed the drive to the polo club.

*

The club was lush with well-watered plantations. It had the peaceful, relaxed atmosphere associated with big animals and rich people. It was also a place to meet interesting persons, make and develop business contacts, and of course, above all, play polo.

The players had gathered in the shade of a gazebo. Grooms were lining up the ponies along the fence in anticipation of the first chukka. As usual, Geoffrey had contrived to be at the centre of attention. He was always trying to look good and important, either chatting up the girls in the hope of an affair or the wealthiest players with whom he might do business. Geoffrey Hutton IV was a pain, but he didn't know it.

As befitted people way up the pecking order of power and money, the patrons of the teams were late. Already dressed up with boots and knee protection, the lower-life players were clustered around Louis or listening to the banter of the Argentinian professionals.

Gusto, Ali's polo manager, was bragging about the merits of his national soccer team, compared of course to those of the English. Under the friendly chat, one could still recognize the after-effects of the Malvinas debacle. Naji imprudently remarked that Argentina had not found an equal successor to Maradona.

"Stand up when you hear the name of Maradona!" roared Gusto to the assembly.

Geoffrey stopped dead in the tirade he was giving to a long-legged blonde. Naji being a wealthy businessman in his own right, Geoffrey changed track and decided to placate business expectations rather than nurture sexual fantasies with Miss Legs. "Don't you think that the UAE national team will soon compete in the final rounds of the World Cup? They have so many good players now."

Naji and the blonde gave Louis a knowing look.

Ali's Ferrari swerved to a stop at the near end of the line of ponies. The head groom walked to meet his boss with shining boots and knee pads in his hands. He kneeled and Ali, one hand on the groom's shoulder, pushed his feet in the boots. We moved towards him to offer our greetings. Ali was one of the major business powers in Dubai and any of us could benefit from his attentions. Geoffrey naturally was at the forefront.

"Come on, guys. Let's play polo!" shouted Ali.

We had already donned the jerseys of our respective teams and we mounted our horses. For the first chukka, I rode my little bay mare. Marzouka was nimble, fast and yet obedient. Light in the hands, she would turn on penny and a pressure of the calves would trigger instant top speed. I loved Marzouka. I was playing number one in the team, in the striker's position usually reserved for the least experienced rider. Ali was our back in number four, Gusto number three. With these two strong players to propel the team, we were assured of a decent showing. Geoffrey was number two in the opposing team, in support of their striker. Naji was their back and Adolfo, the other Argie, their number three. Miss Legs and the other spectators left the gazebo to take a seat along the edge of the pitch.

*

Knowledgeable people claim that polo gives the best possible high with one's clothes on. I wholeheartedly agreed.

The game developed into a stalemate, the strong players at the back of each team being too good for their weaker attacking opponents. At a slow canter, Ali, Naji and the Argie pros were thwarting our efforts and the game flowed fruitlessly from one end of the pitch to the other.

The first chukka was coming to an end when Geoffrey found himself clear in the right corner of his team's goal line. All our players had been on the attack. The ball died on Louis' off side. A lucky stroke propelled the ball sixty meters towards our goal and Geoffrey set off at full speed with a clear run for scoring ahead of him. I was the nearest player and I squeezed Marzouka's flanks with a yell. The mare felt the urgency and responded with joy. We charged, two lengthening strides behind Geoffrey, as his head start had given him the advantage of the impetus and acceleration.

A polo pitch is three hundred meters long. A good polo pony gallops at three hundred and fifty to four hundred meters a minute. Fifty seconds to stop Geoffrey. Sensing his opportunity for glory, Geoffrey gave it all he had. His horse was from Naji's stable and was a good one too. After fifty meters, the gap between us reduced to three strides. Leaning forward along the horse's neck, I yelled in the fashion of Johnny Reb—to vent my excitement, to urge Marzouka further and to rattle Geoffrey whose back was taunting me ten meters away. At the same time I was rhythmically thumping my legs against the flanks of my pony. Brave horse! I could feel her body stretching further at each stride forward. We were gaining! Now I was one-and-a-half strides behind! But a quick glance towards our goal line showed we were a mere hundred meters away!

I kicked harder, l leaned lower, I yelled louder and Geoffrey made his mistake. He looked over his shoulder and lost a fraction of his momentum. I made up one stride. Now we were almost in shooting range. Geoffrey lifted his mallet behind him. Again the movement caused him to lose another quantum of momentum. I squeezed all I could from a now near-winded Marzouka and came to contact with my right knee just behind Geoffrey's left leg. Marzouka's shoulder gave enough push to unsettle his stroke and the ball rolled under his mount. Ali, galloping close behind us, hit a strong back hander to clear the danger. Geoffrey straightened in his saddle: "Why did you do this to me?" he screeched "I could have scored!"

*

As we walked our ponies back to the tethering line Geoffrey was moaning. He was annoyed at having been undone in plain sight of Miss Legs. "We should cooperate, Jon," he said, "rather than spoil it for each other. Actually, I've got a nice proposal for you. You shouldn't put me in a mind to change your luck."

I had had my fun. There was no point ramming in that I actually out-rode him in a straight man-to-man challenge. I knew I would cherish the memory of that ride for a while and I could afford to be magnanimous. We handed over the horses to the waiting grooms and walked back towards the gazebo and the spectators.

"I was just plain lucky, Geoffrey. And Marzouka has a good turn of speed. Polo business is polo business, right? Let's have a drink together at the Blue Note after the game and you tell me all about your scheme: you know me, silent like a fish and industrious as an ant."

"Done," replied Geoffrey. "Aperitif on me at seven-thirty. And be gentle with an old guy in the next chukka. You don't have to gallop your horse to death each time someone is likely to score against you." With a wink he sat down next to the shapely blonde. I winked back at Geoffrey and smiled at the lady before turning to Ali and Gusto to receive their teasing compliments on my undoing of Geoffrey's charge down the field.

*

The game had been lively with a final score of 5 to 3 in our favor. I had scored a dicey goal with a good long shot under the neck which, added to the race with Geoffrey, made for a satisfying afternoon. A shower at the polo field had not removed the strangely delectable stiffness in my limbs and back. I parked the convertible in the basement of the Ibis Hotel and took the lift to the bar.

Geoffrey and Miss Legs were sitting in the far corner of the room. He waived at me and I sat down in front of them. A pianist was playing soft background music. A smiling waitress took my order for a cold beer and I stretched my legs with a sigh of comfort. Geoffrey's companion was looking at me with a friendly squint. Geoffrey, however, wanted my attention.

"Naji trusts your judgment, does he not?"

"Why, yes indeed."

"Would he take your advice on a large investment?"

"Why would he want my opinion?" I asked, somewhat surprised at the unusual angle of this conversation.

"Leave that to me," said Geoffrey, "but if he asks, can you convince him?"

"Convince him about what, Geoffrey? Please stop talking in riddles!"

Geoffrey had a sip of beer and moved in his seat. He was obviously looking for a way to get my help without telling me the whole story. "Look," he finally said, "I'm masterminding a unique investment opportunity. Guaranteed forty percent internal rate of return. I need financial muscle to get that going: five million dollars. Help me line that up and I'll get you a three percent commission when the funds are available. Naji has spare cash and I know my proposal is right down his line of interest. What do you say?"

"What do I say? What line of business is it? And how come I should be able to influence his judgment? In the first place I would want to convince myself."

"Jon, you're an engineer. You're sincere and genuine. Naji will want a qualified view. He will take your word. Here is a copy of the business plan I gave him. Read it and when he asks, give him an honest opinion. He will ask you. Leave it to me to make sure he does. Deal?"

Geoffrey raised his glass, flashing a big smile all around, particularly towards Miss Legs. I finished my beer and stood up to take my leave, the folder under my arm. Geoffrey shook my hand with glee. His companion held my grip a fraction of a second longer than strictly necessary.

"My name is Katherina," she said. Her smile was well worth the effort of listening to Geoffrey, no matter what was in the folder.

*

The week dragged slowly on. At last it was Thursday. I could begin to think of leisure and the weekend, away from the grind of the chemical company which benefitted from my exertions.

A call from Geoffrey came as a pleasant diversion. "Jon? Have you read my business plan? What you say?"

I had been through the folder over the previous two evenings. The scheme was simple enough. Geoffrey had found in Germany a second-hand factory for the manufacture of prefabricated wall panels. There was a huge demand in Dubai for all building materials. Compared with procuring a new one, the factory was for sale at a fraction of the going rate. Buying this low-cost factory, guaranteed to be in perfect working condition, made the project a winner from the start since the depreciation charges would be a fraction of the cost to the competition.

Why there should be such an astonishing and exceptional opportunity wasn't really for me to judge or to question. If the purchase was possible at that ridiculously low price, then it was somebody's good luck. Why not Geoffrey's and Naji's?

"Sounds good, Geoffrey. Why would you need me to convince Naji?" As I said that, I thought I knew the reason already: Geoffrey was known for his bullish sales manners and his poor after-sales service. The continuation of the conversation was predictable.

"Jon, you know why. Naji trusts you. You're an honest engineer and your opinion will have lots of weight in his final decision. Tell you what: give me a written appraisal of the business plan. A one-page summary or less is OK. Address it to me and I'll take it from there." I remained silent as he went on, pleading: "Listen, Jon. Make an effort: writing what I need will not take more than half an hour of your time. You will be my partner. The figures speak for themselves. Either you believe simple arithmetic or you don't. The offer of the seller is genuine, and there is nothing else to it. Do it please. I will ask Katherina to pick it up at your flat tonight. 9pm is OK?"

I wasn't much inclined to condone Geoffrey's business machinations. Yet business is business. I had bills to meet, rent to cough up, installments on the convertible, and livery stables to pay. Plus there was the prospect of Katherina's visit. Perhaps she would smile again.

"OK, Geoffrey. I'll do it. The offer of second-hand equipment is genuine, yes? Did you check the condition of the equipment? it's readily operational?"

Geoffrey was quick to reassure me: "Of course yes! You can trust me, Jon. Katherina will be there at nine. I will give her your mobile number just in case. Ciao."

"Ciao, Geoffrey." I was at the same time despondent to find myself associated with Geoffrey's activities against my will, and vaguely elated at the thought of seeing Miss Legs again.

I left early and went back to my flat to finish off the report intended for Naji.

*

Nine-thirty pm. I had worked steadily since getting home and had wrapped up a neat analysis of the business proposal. With an internal rate of return in excess of 45% and break-even sales at 12% of the plant capacity, there was hardly a doubt about the merits of the proposal. The letter addressed to Geoffrey was ready and I poured myself a glass of white wine.

My mobile rang at ten o'clock. The throaty yet sweet Russian voice of Katherina enquired whether I was home and had the document expected by Geoffrey. As I confirmed both, she said she would be ringing my bell in five minutes. I hung up and rushed to the bathroom to brush my teeth. I placed two glasses and the chilled bottle of white wine on the coffee table. I had a teasing sense of anticipation below the belt as the bell rang. I rushed to the door with a big smile. Katherina smiled in return but in response to my inviting sweep of the arm, didn't move from the door step. "Have you got the report? Geoffrey asked me to bring an original, please."

"Yes of course." What else could I say to such an alluring lady? I handed her the envelope. She shook my hand as a queen would, or so I felt. Again the contact lasted a fraction longer than a mere handshake, but it was hardly a consolation for the prospect of finishing the wine alone and placing the second glass back in the kitchen cabinet unused.

2. Katherina's Friends

Jon

Several days went by with no news from Geoffrey, no news from Naji and no polo. I refrained from calling anyone, for fear of appearing too eager. I was slowly driving home after another long day at the office. The ring of the mobile phone was a welcome interruption of my reverie.

"Jon? How are you keeping?"

Katherina's voice immediately restored some of my natural pep. "Hi, Katherina! I'm fine! What about you? Long time no see."

"I'm all right, Jon. Nice to talk to you. Geoffrey sends his thanks. How busy are you tomorrow night?"

That was an evening I would need to finish my monthly activity report, but then what is a report when there is an alluring blonde in the balance?

"Actually I'm free as a bird, Katherina."

"Good," she said, "then would you like to meet a couple of friends of mine? There may be some interesting business for you down the line. I pick you up at your place say 7pm?"

"With pleasure. Is this a formal occasion?" I asked, hoping for details.

"Not at all," she replied. "My friends are simple, straightforward people. You will like them. Seven o'clock then. That's settled. Good night, Jon! See you."

Again the lingering friendliness. I felt cheered up. Back at my place, I opened the draft report on my laptop and got to work in earnest so that I could keep the next day free for whatever Katherina had in store for me.

I went to bed, fantasizing.

*

Again the day dragged in slow motion. Routine emails and faxes, quotations, presentations of products, the face of Katherina popping up every once in a while. The office boy brought tasteless coffee. Only five minutes gone since the last time I looked at the clock.

At long last the sweeping hand reached the top at 5pm and I could switch off my laptop, wave at my colleagues, say bye to the receptionist lady and disappear from the working stage.

*

Back at home, I had a cool shower, brushed my teeth, donned a smart T-shirt, and went back to my favorite past-time of the day, watching the hands of my clock creeping towards the blessed time of 7 o'clock. It took forever and then nothing happened. But then, one should have some tolerance towards a lady's appreciation of time. I watched TV for a while, unable to concentrate on what I was seeing. I read through an uninspiring magazine without a single word registering in my brain. Coffee didn't help.

And then the miracle. At 8.15, the phone rang and the heavenly, raunchy voice of Katherina enquired whether I was home and ready. Of course I was. Could she pick me up in ten minutes? Of course she could.

And I set about waiting once again. And waiting. By ten past nine, the phone rang. She was downstairs, waiting for me in her car. By then I was fuming.

Her car was a dark blue Aston Martin, of James Bond fame. I felt a pinch of envy, thinking of the many installments still due on my red job. She drove expertly and smoothly through the traffic of Al Wasl Road, towards the posh end of Jumeirah. The bulky silhouette of the Burj Al Arab profiled itself against the night sky. From the corner of my eye, I could see Katherina's long legs moving as she drove. My wrath was melting.

"Where are we going?" I asked without much elaboration, just to show that I had been annoyed.

She flashed a big smile and my anger disappeared entirely. "Boris has a room in the Burj Al Arab. We will meet him and his partners in the hotel."

I relaxed back in the leather seat, one eye on the legs and the other on the road. The Burj Al Arab—the Arab tower—is spectacular, it's a spectacle by itself. Its mass dominates the landscape for miles. Clever shifting lights create a feel of motionless movement in the body of the construction, huge yet balanced and harmonious. Tonight there was a soft orange light caressing the bulge of the structural fabric that contained the 200-meter-high volume of the hotel lobby.

We passed security with only a smile at the guard. There was an unobtrusive tag on the windshield. The car glided along the smooth curve of the bridge linking the Burj with Jumeirah Beach Road. The hotel grew bigger and bigger until it was no longer possible to capture it to its full height. Katherina swerved in front of the entrance and doormen, valets and porters set about justifying the seven stars of their establishment.

Every time I had walked into the Burj Al Arab, the majestic volume of the hotel lobby had caught my breath and again I couldn't take my eyes away from the magnet of the enormous space stretching upwards to a height of over fifty floors. The curved walls of the rooms, cleverly extending into the rails of the passageways above, made the lounge look like a giant beehive.

We took the escalator to the upper level of the lobby, which gave me an opportunity to look lower down, standing behind Katherina. She turned around and noticed my looking at her legs. I blushed. The corridor to the bank of lifts was decorated in lavish bright red-blue-green mosaics, turning into lush carpet with sumptuous colors in the red tones. The lift cabin was large, decorated with gold. Its motion was silky.

Smiling at me, Katherina rang the bell of suite 1702. Obviously this was a good moment for her. And why not? She was beautiful, in one of the most luxurious environments on the planet, in the company of a handsome young man (no reason for me to be bashful about it), and about to meet a rich friend. I returned the smile, largely for the same reasons. The door opened a bit and a pert dark face appeared in the crack. Long black hair surrounded the pretty smiling features.

"Hi, I'm Hope," said the cute face, opening the door, nodding to Katherina and stretching a manicured hand in my direction. I grabbed a limp bundle of unresponsive fingers, which I shook in pretence of manners.

"Good evening. I'm Jon, Jonny to my friends," I replied encouragingly.

Hope wasn't to be encouraged. She turned around and moved back into suite 1702. We followed on the thick carpet and entered the lounge. The furniture was lacquered in soft grey colors with gold inlay. The sofa and deep armchairs were in soft dark grey leather. The fluffy lilac drapes matched the purple undertones of the carpeting to give a feel of utter coziness. The window offered a wide view of the Arabian Gulf (may God help the uncouth foreigner who mistakenly calls it Persian Gulf). Lights on the Palm Island were flickering in the distance.

A burly man, bald, mid-thirties, dressed in a fashionable open-neck T-shirt and slacks, appeared at the top of the curving stairs that led to the upper floor of the duplex suite. Katherina gave him a hug as he reached the lounge and she introduced me. Boris obviously. We sat in the leather chairs, Hope nesting against the bulk of our host.

Boris was used to being the centre of attention. He took control with aplomb and said in a gravelly voice: "Jon, Katherina tells me you're a dependable and honest person. I need your help. Nothing special, but I have little time. I fly back to Moscow after two days. Here are two hundred and fifty thousand dollars in cash." He placed an envelope on the low table in front of him. "I want you to go and buy some gold. I have been told there is a gold market here. Go there and buy what you find as a good bargain. Diamonds as well.

Actually, you can buy more diamonds. Less weight to carry, hey!" He laughed at his wit and in his mirth slapped Hope on the thigh. "And, by the way, you can keep five thousand dollars for yourself for your work. Bring me receipts for the purchases, yes?"

I was puzzled. I knew people like Boris existed, but I had never met one in the flesh. Was all this legal? On the other hand, five thousand dollars was welcome, what with Marzouka and the car installments. And the job did not appear difficult or dangerous.

Katherina smiled encouragingly. Hope was watching her nails. Boris went to the lacquered bar and poured shots of iced vodka for everybody. "Good, Jon. It is done then. Here is the money." He pushed the envelope across the table. "No need for receipt. Katherina's word is good enough for me. You bring to Katherina tomorrow evening, yes?"

That was a bit fast for me, but then five K are five K. What the hell. This didn't sound like hard-core criminality and if it was money laundering, then so be it. I never had that much reverence for the establishment in the first place.

I slipped the brown envelope in the back pocket of my jeans. We all drank vodka. "To the meeting and friendship of Jon and Boris!" Boris was delighted with his hospitality, manners and business. As he raised his glass again, the door opened and a tall muscular man walked in, escorted by two dark beauties from Hope's mold.

Boris reveled in the increased attendance and lined up more vodka glasses. "Meet my friend Vladimir! You can call him Vlad! And here are Faith and Charity. This is how we work for the salvation of our souls! We practice cardinal virtues, ha, ha, ha!" To underline his meaning, Boris whacked the nearest virtue on her bottom. The three Filipinas laughed politely to acknowledge the sense of humor of their temporary employer, if employer was the right word in the circumstances.

We drank to Russia, to the United Arab Emirates, to the Philippines and its female population, to the view of the Persian Gulf, to the Burj al Arab and to my employer when I disclosed my professional activities. By then I was feeling very unsteady on my legs. Katherina had a knowing look and intervened with tact. "Jon, we will get you a limo from the front desk to take you home. I have to stay a bit for some work with Boris. You will be OK."

"Some work?" I thought with a bit of envy. Never mind. I had had too much vodka and retiring gracefully was my best option. Katherina took me to the front desk to arrange the billing of the limo on Boris's room. On the way she told me that Geoffrey was very happy with my appraisal of the German factory business plan, and that I would hear from him soon.

Sitting on the posh back seat of the hotel limousine as it glided airily through the night down Jumeirah Beach road, I felt somewhat depressed despite the improbable bulk of a quarter of a million dollars against my buttock.

I had been used, and I was drunk.

3. Geoffrey's Scam

Katherina

Hope and Faith, the two preferred cardinal virtues of Boris, were about to leave the suite when the bell rang. Trust Jon for being on time. The fool was so eager that he was early. Never mind, he could make what he wanted of the presence of the two girls.

I liked their smooth golden skin. Still childlike in some ways, they had spontaneous manners and no hang ups. Their laughter was clear and they had no inhibitions. We had been in bed, all three of us, for an early holy siesta.

There was hardly time enough for a touch of makeup and tidying my wig before opening the door. Jon cast a perplexed look at the disheveled appearance of the two girls, as they walked past him out of the hotel suite. He stood awkwardly in the doorway.

"Come in, Jon," I said. "We have a few minutes. You care for a coffee or a glass of wine?" He opted for a coffee.

I had to put some spine into Geoffrey's deal. I gave Jon a peck on the cheek. It amused me to see him blush again. Now, with Boris, we had assessed that Jon was sensitive to money. He was also helplessly attracted to my figure. If only he knew!

Using one incentive or the other to clinch the deal was up to me, but Boris wanted to go back to Moscow and he was getting impatient. Geoffrey had failed to finalize the deal with Naji, and Boris wanted to close the subject before leaving. The seller of the second-hand factory was a contact of Boris's. Geoffrey was involved, not because of his reputation as an astute broker which existed only in his own mind, but because of his contact with Naji. Boris also needed a fall guy. Boris's Dutch correspondent had approached Geoffrey through the network of diplomatic representations. The plant in fact was a derelict unit from a dismantled facility in East Germany.

The mathematics of the scam was simple. The actual commercial value of the plant was just about its weight in scrap: the cast iron of the machine frames, the copper in the cables and electric motors. Probable value half a million dollars at best. Geoffrey had been briefed that a new similar factory would cost sixteen million. This one was available for a mere five million.

I told Louis to insist on being a twenty percent partner to Naji's eighty percent. I assured the usually indebted Geoffrey that I would persuade Boris to fund his venture. Knowing Boris's thoughts and methods, I expected that when the Naji/Geoffrey partnership paid five millions US to the Dutch seller, one million would go to the original owner in Leipzig and four would come back to Boris. Of these four, one had to repay the advance given to Geoffrey as bait, and about half a million would go to cover expenses such as my fee and that of the Dutch front man. Not bad for a simple introduction exploiting the gullibility and greed of a few people. Whether the factory ever worked was immaterial to Boris.

Geoffrey had no secrets from me after I had not-so-inadvertently placed my hand on his thigh. He told me all about his investment plans and soon he was seeking my advice. Boris's plan was developing better than Geoffrey's.

Except for Naji's slow decision making. Jon made an impression with his initial report. Geoffrey, however, had failed to nail the deal. I had to engineer a push.

Jon was gingerly holding out a bulky bag, his arm straining under the weight of it. "Here," he said. "I have been at the gold souk and spent Boris's money. I hope he likes my choices. The receipts are inside." I took the bag, heavy indeed. Jon had been diligent and honest as expected. Good. Time for the next move.

"I have a secret to share with you, Jon," I said. "I feel I can trust you. Will you help me?"

Full of fervor, he dutifully replied: "Sure, Katherina. I want to help you. Any time. All the time if you allow me." It was punctuated with a blush.

Now that was bold of him! "It's a simple thing, Jon. Geoffrey is so keen on the deal with Naji that he has promised me a good fee if he can pull it off. I need that money, Jon. Can you convince Naji? Please?" I handed him a glass of the white wine I had been sharing with the two virtues.

I could still see the flickering light of uncertainty in Jon's eyes. "My parents live in Kiev. My father has cancer and he needs very expensive drugs. Being a personal assistant to Boris does not make me rich, not even comfortable. Everything you see here, even my clothes, belong to Boris. He does not pay that much, you know. He wants me near him and looking good only for show. I need all the help I can get, Jon." My hand was on his arm. I could feel his tenseness.

Then he relaxed and said: "Only Naji can convince Naji. However, if Geoffrey can give me solid data about the status of the second-hand plant—like pictures, a third party inspection report, maintenance records, whatever—I will do my bit and repeat my earlier advice to Naji, with a positive appraisal of the plant if I can back it up."

Better. I was sure Boris could line up a bogus inspection report from a so-called quality assurance company in no time at all. We would get cracking on it right away. "Thanks, Jon. Geoffrey will be delighted and I'm very, very grateful to you. Let me call Geoffrey and give him the good news." I grabbed the mobile phone and gave Jon another peck on the cheek. His lucky day, no doubt.

Geoffrey was unfamiliar with the duties and routines of inspection companies. I couldn't tell him in front of Jon that I was certain to get the inspection report. So I decided to leave explanations for later and, closing the phone, turned back to Jon with the required dose of self-assurance: "He will get the report very soon. Let's go and meet Naji. We may be late for the meeting."

Jon finished his coffee and walked to the window. The sea was deep blue. A dinghy was sailing in the distance, bouncing on the short swell, her ludicrous pinkish sails bobbing with the waves.

We left the room. Jon was my hostage.

*

The polo club was still quiet when we arrived. Gusto was allocating horses to players on the back of an envelope. Grooms started saddling horses under his instructions. Birds were flying around the pounds near the gazebo. The lawn was springy under our feet.

We had just reached the pergola when Naji's car entered the car park. Protocol was saved. It is bad manners to keep a big shot waiting.

Naji was cheerful enough. "Hi Katherina! Hi Jon! Ready to play?" I could tell from his friendly tap on Jon's shoulder that he liked and trusted the young man. We sat down, watching the peaceful scenery. From time to time a horse would wag its tail to keep flies away. The grooms were wrapping protective bandages around the legs of the ponies.

"You have something to add to your report, Jon?" Naji was getting down to business. Jon looked at me. I held his gaze with an encouraging smile and pouting lips. He gave me an uncertain smirk in return.

"The feasibility of the project is good, very good even." Jon was warming to his subject. "With the market we have now, the whole business depends on the plant being in good shape and reliable."

"So?" asked Naji.

"There is the crux of the matter. That is what you ought to verify. Short of going there and seeing for yourself, you could appoint an agency to report on the status of the machinery. Delegating the task may be the better option since a technical background and expertise in the field is advisable. The agency could also give you a report of past activities and performance. In this way, you would have a direct and independent confirmation of the business plan."

I could see that Jon's little speech had made an impact. Naji was thinking. I smiled at Jon. It was high time however to get things moving in the right direction. I opted for boldness and said: "Listen, you guys, you seem to be going round in circles. Why don't you just go there, both of you? This is no business of mine, but if you have questions, go where the answers are."

I could see the wheels spinning in Naji's mind. All we needed now was Geoffrey to make a travel plan to Naji's liking. I was confident Boris would fund Jon's journey. And Boris would organize a convincing inspection.

4. The Plant in Hamburg

Geoffrey

Katherina took charge of our lot and our plans. In the space of two days she had organized the meeting with the seller, a Schengen visa for Naji, the tickets and the hotels. The plant had been dismantled, packed in 17 containers and held in transit in the yard of a major German freight forwarder. And not only had she convinced Naji and Jon to make the trip, when I requested her to join the party, she agreed at once.

The lounge of the Hamburg Hilton was busy. Intent businessmen clustered at a low table covered with documents, talking in hurried tones. A group of Americans passed by, recognizable by their trousers upturned half an inch higher than the rest of the world. A lone hooker was seated in a corner of the lounge, waiting for trade. Naji had swapped the dishdash of the Arabian Gulf for a Brioni suit and a bright pink tie. Katherina was stunning as always, in a dark grey suit which enhanced her silhouette. The cream shirt, a pearl necklace and matching ear-rings relieved the severity of her appearance. The top three buttons of her shirt were undone, inviting attention. Jon, his usual dynamic self, was speculating on the arrival of the Dutch seller of the plant. True to form for Middle East VIPs and women used to luxury, our party had taken most of the morning just to get out of bed and assemble on the lounge sofas.

Jon was raring to go: "He should be here! It will take at least an hour to get to the storage area. Checking the plant will take at least fifteen minutes per container, what with the packing lists and identifying each item. Maybe more. And where is the guy from the inspection company?"

To be on the safe side, as suggested by Katherina, I had mobilized the inspection agency she had recommended to verify the consignment alongside our team. I had briefly wondered how she could possibly have all these contacts. She was so gorgeous, efficient and knowledgeable. What a woman! With a bit of luck, the intimacy of traveling together and staying in the same hotel could develop into bedding her. I put a hand on her arm in response to Jon's outburst of impatience: "Darling, the agency's inspector is due to meet us at noon, right? And so is Mr Vanhoof." And then to Jon: "It is hardly 15 minutes past 12, Jon. Traffic here is as bad as in any big city. Give them a chance." I had a quick glance at Naji, whose patience was a lot more important to me than Jon's. I smiled reassuringly at him and then back to Katherina: "Would you give them a call, darling, just to be sure."

Katherina obliged and reported that Mr Vanhoof and the inspector were parking their car. Soon they walked in. Mr Vanhoof was a portly, smiling man with gold spectacles and affable manners. The inspector, tall and stern, breathed authority and purposefulness. Naji shook hands and suggested we get going to make most of the day. Mr Vanhoof mobilized a stretched limo with a driver for our party and as we drove off he started a running commentary on the history and monuments of Hamburg. Dark green church domes dotted the skyline. Naji was polite.

The city seemed to stretch out a long way. Gradually the density of constructions thinned. More trees and gardens appeared and the road became narrower. Our mentor mentioned lunch and suggested a welcoming inn on the way. Katherina said she was hungry. Jon, sitting in front, couldn't protest. Naji couldn't turn down hospitality. The agency man frowned at the professional laxity, but being paid by hour, couldn't care less.

I was concerned with the timetable, but if Naji agreed, then so be it. I was hoping that the visit would not be too long, so that I could lose Naji and Jon in the notorious Reeperbahn in the evening and have Katherina all to myself.

The limo glided into a graveled car park next to a large mansion that had a huge stone staircase in front. Glistening luxury cars in the parking lot exuded solid wealth and cozy comfort.

The maitre d' of the gasthof was expecting us and he steered our group to a round table surrounded by windows and overlooking a park. Mr Vanhoof insisted on champagne to welcome his guests. Naji stuck to orange juice. Mr Vanhoof then insisted on entrees. Naji made sure that there was no pork in his sausages. Straight-faced, Vanhoof confirmed there was none. After the Riesling, we got into a red wine of the Black Forest to accompany the "plat de resistance". Skipping the dessert wasn't possible, so we indulged in Viennese pastries. But then Naji put his foot down. He had displayed manners and patience as required from a willing guest, but business couldn't wait any longer. Mr Vanhoof sighed at the thought of missing coffee, cognac and cigars.

We reached the storage yard by 4pm. The manager of the depot fussed around, offered coffee and displayed sheaves of photocopies. Katherina attempted to translate. Both Naji and Jon wanted to see the goods, not the paperwork, and be done with it. With eyes on Katherina's décolleté and my mind on the prospect of my fee, I added my voice to the plea for moving on. The manager picked a register, called for a worker and they drove off in front of us. Containers were stacked six-high, leaving narrow passages for traffic. It wasn't unlike Manhattan without the crowds. They drove for a long time. There wasn't thing to differentiate this stack of containers bar the manager, pointing at the numbers on his list.

Containers have double doors at one end. To open the doors, the containers of the next stack had to be taken out of the way. Also, our dignified inspector wasn't likely to levitate in order to access the containers above ground level. Mr Vanhoof had a chat with the yard manager and turned to our perplexed group to announce that a forklift was on the way. He suggested we get back in the limo and be a little patient till the containers were made accessible.

There was no choice. The first container was on the ground and open well past 6 o'clock. By then, even the prolific Mr Vanhoof had run out of conversation. As the forklift operator opened the double doors, we filed out of the limo and assembled in the gathering dusk as if in front of an altar. The steel assemblies were packed tight within the walls of the container. Only a squirrel would be capable of getting in and, short of unpacking it, it was difficult to make sense of what we saw. Some parts were gleaming in the fading light. Others were painted dark blue. The yard manager pointed at a tally sheet and gave a long explanation that Mr Vanhoof translated.

"This container carries two bending machines and a shear. You can see the end of the shear. Come and have a look!" He waived us closer, proud of his goods and keen to have us share the eagerness.

The inspection and verification task would require days. We were wasting our time. We turned to our austere inspecting companion and Naji took charge. "You will give us a report, then. How long is it likely to take?"

At last, the inspector was in the limelight. He relished the recognition of his importance. He turned to Mr Vanhoof: "I will need a forklift and a team of three workers for three or four days." And turning to Naji: "You will then have my report one week later. I can start tomorrow if the help is available."

Mr Vanhoof was beaming: "Sure. You will have your team tomorrow morning. We will wait for your report."

There was a sense of relief in the group as the tedium of the inspection had been passed down the line, to a party better qualified and equipped. There was a vague feeling of guilt at the small size of our achievements, mixed with the satisfaction of having confirmed the existence of the plant. It was time to plan the more pleasant side of the evening.

*

I managed to send Naji on a sightseeing tour which included the famed Reeperbahn. Perhaps he already intended to go, given the propensity of Middle Eastern men to seek flesh spots when away from the constraints of their milieu. In any case, he didn't need much prompting. My luck held good as Naji invited Jon to accompany him. Katherina was mine to entertain for the evening.

I selected the best restaurant of the hotel so that there would be no disruptive commuting between the preparation and the exploitation phases. Only the best champagne would do and we had oysters as starters, I was hoping that their properties would have the right effect on my companion. Katherina was cheerful and had a healthy appetite. She laughed at my jokes and exercised her wit with no holding back. She was wearing a designer red dress with a simple gold chain. Her hair was held in a bun, the graceful line of her neck on full display.

As we waited for the Chateaubriand, a pensive moment came at a low in our conversation. The time was ripe for a first move and I placed my hand across the table on her naked forearm. She smiled and kept her arm in place. Her flesh was smooth as silk. Just as I hoped to push my advantage, she pulled her arm away. The contact had been long enough to give hope, and short enough not to give too much. "I like you, Geoffrey," she said, "but we need time. Feelings must be free to grow without pressure." She punctuated the statement with a pat on my errant hand.

I had to be content with that. She declined dessert and another drink at the hotel disco. I still had a faint hope that she would allow me to accompany her to her room door, on the same floor as mine. The hope died with: "Good night, Geoffrey. It was a lovely evening. I hope we can have more wonderful times like this again." I got a quick kiss on the cheek and was left staring at a door.

*

I passed a bad night. Drinking two neat whiskies by myself to dull the frustration didn't help me sleep and I twisted around in the bed for a long time before I managed a short slumber. I woke up at 7 o'clock next morning with a dry mouth and a pouncing throb in my head. I gave myself the regulation triple-S and left the room, heading for the coffee shop, as a pot of coffee appeared to be the one remedy I needed most.

As I closed the room door I saw a man looking like our dear Mr Vanhoof enter the lift, although, seeing him from the back, I wasn't one hundred percent sure. What could he be doing on this floor? With Katherina?

The coffee didn't taste good.

5. The Party

Geoffrey

I couldn't keep it to myself. I was going to be rich! No more petty restraints, no more kowtows to unworthy characters. Finished the pernickety administration, gone the supercilious "chef de cabinet". I had to celebrate.

I called all my acquaintances. The secretary of the office sent invitations to every single individual whose hand I had shaken in the previous two years. I now expected some two hundred guests to a buffet dinner near the pool of my residence. A couple of my usual cronies—Jon for one—appeared somewhat glum when I rang him, but nothing could restrain my glee. Of course Naji would be there, although I would not let him know that he was the primary reason for my bliss. Mr Vanhoof was in town, no doubt to cash in the letter of credit, and he would be coming to the party as well. Perhaps even Ali would attend and if not him, Gusto would, with the rest of the polo gang.

Katherina was bringing my contribution to the capital of Naji's venture in the form of a one-million-dollar cheque. I had persuaded her to bring along her mysterious Russian mentor, and I was still hopeful of overcoming her not-so-virtuous resistance. In any case a number of ladies of unequal virtue were also on the guest list, and as the story goes, some were more unequal than others. There would always be an opportunity of sorts.

The celebrations had the added advantage of being paid for through an expense account. The Ministry would squeak a little, but the raison d'état was on my side.

*

The crowd slowly built up around the pool. Self-conscious Indian businessmen, firmly conventional in their attire and manners, and keen to a fault; Arab youngsters in daring designer casuals; locals in traditional garb; women in dazzling evening dresses; Westerners in T-shirts (the sporty mob) or jacket and tie (the business pack); Iranians and expatriate Arabs in shirt without tie in the new Middle East style—the crowd was as diverse as Dubai itself. No local ladies though. Parties are not for them. Not this type of party in any case.

Naji, having at long last issued the five-million-dollar letter of credit, was the object of my considerate attention. After the courtesies de rigueur I took him to Katherina and her group. This was my first meeting with her boss. Boris was his name and he fitted the bill to perfection: a burly hunk of a man, lots of flashy rings, a glittering necklace hanging in an open shirt, expensive casual clothing, golden teeth and an overpowering demeanor. A couple of tough-looking un-smiling guys stood at his shoulders. He took over the conversation with Naji and I pulled Katherina away.

"Nice party, Geoffrey. Good to see you again."

I was determined to enjoy the feeling of success and make the most of my luck: "You're stunning tonight, as always. How come we never see you with a boyfriend?"

She made a nonchalant gesture, as if chasing away an importune fly. "Why would I need a boyfriend when you're there for me, Geoffrey? You're attentive, solicitous, well mannered and good looking."

Smiling, the bitch had placed a hand on my arm and was giving me a gentle squeeze. Was she taunting me again? "Thanks, Katherina. Nice of you to recognize my attention. But I need more of you in my life, you know. Could we have an evening together? Champagne dinner here if you wish. The two of us. Or better still, stay here tonight and we'll celebrate this deal together!"

"Some time, Geoffrey, give me some time." I had to be content with that. She went on, "Congratulations on the deal, though. I understand Naji has opened the letter of credit and the goods are about to be delivered. You have signed the shareholders' agreement with Naji, yes? And when will you pay your share of the capital to Naji? I have the cheque here with me."

The one-million-dollar loan from Boris which would pay for my share in Naji's new business was going to be released against so many deeds, undertakings, pledges and agreements in favor of Boris, all to be signed and sealed, that sometimes I wondered if I was going to be rich after all. Well now was too late or too early to worry. "Can we have a moment later in the evening for you to sign the receipt and the other papers? The cheque is too heavy for me to carry." Again the teasing smile.

I had to turn to greet Mr Vanhoof as he came in with a large smile and outstretched hand. He pulled me away for a quick aparté. "Congratulations, Mr Hutton," he said. "We now have a fair win-win deal, profitable to all parties. May I ask a last favor?" I nodded and he continued: "Could you ensure with Mr Naji that the LC payment be made promptly and without hassle, if you can. The ship will offload tomorrow. The bill of lading and the survey are available at the Dubai Commercial Bank."

Well, we were all keen, but his impatience somewhat surprised me.

A young local in a dishdash introduced himself and we shook hands: "Thanks for your invitation, Mr Hutton. My name is Rashed. You have organized a pleasant evening and I'm grateful to be with you tonight." The man's face was vaguely familiar, but I did not recall the name on the list of invitees. Never mind, a local is always a potential for business so I played along. He turned to Mr Vanhoof and politely enquired about his business in Dubai. I moved away to greet more guests and have a better look at what company I could marshal to finish the night's celebration in my bed if Katherina didn't oblige. But business is business and she still had to hand over the cheque.

*

At last, the party settled down. No more latecomers to greet. Most guests had helped themselves to the buffet. Groups had formed and people were engaged in polite inconsequential conversations. I signaled Katherina and, picking up two glasses of champagne from a waiter, preceded her into my study.

She stood near the desk whilst I pretended to examine the sheaf of documents accompanying the cheque. I had read the drafts before and didn't have much choice in any case: it was sign or nothing. As I read the papers her perfume was slowly getting to my head and, shall I say, other parts of my body. The door between my study and the bedroom was slightly open and I could see a corner of the inviting bed.

I signed with a flourish, stood up and handed her a glass for a toast to our success. She took a sip and smiled. As she was placing the glass back on my desk, I made my move. I grabbed her waist with my left arm and pulled her to me for a kiss. She was surprisingly strong and resisted, placing a hand on my chest. However, the drinks, the perfume and the exultation of success had taken over. Somehow — struggling, dragging, pulling, wrestling — I got her through the door and she fell backwards on the bed. She was pinned under my weight. Still seeking the lips from her twisting head, I fondled her with my right hand.

I forced my fingers between her legs, into frilly panties and to my horror found a set of male accessories, belying her — or his? — seductively feminine appearance. I took three steps back, staring at her — him — with complete bewilderment. She — he — stood up, straightened her — his — dress with the back of the hand and walked out of the room, through the study where she — he — picked up the documents and disappeared.

I heard something like "Asshole!" as she walked past.

6. The Falling Cards

Geoffrey

The last three days had been good despite the amorous set-back with that bitch Katherina — or was she a rabid dog? Anyway, the money was in, as Mr Vanhoof had gleefully reported. I was the owner of 20% of a new industrial venture bound to generate millions over the near future and I still had the memory of the soft body which had comforted me at the end of the party. A charming person, she was, with the improbable name of Charity. If charity was about sharing, she sure shared enough and I was looking forward to more of it. The memory of her breasts was lingering in the palms of my hands.

I wasn't happy, though, with the call from that local character Rashed who for all I knew had gate-crashed my party. He mentioned that he was an executive in the Ministry of the Interior and wanted to see me. He would not say why. He also bullied me into accepting a meeting in the late afternoon, precisely at the time when I had arranged for a visit by the delightful and not-so-virtuous bearer of that virtuous name. But turning down potential business is bad business, and turning down a local is bad manners. For a diplomat, even if borderline, it's undiplomatic. So here I was, sipping absurdly strong and overpriced coffee at a ubiquitous Starbuck's joint, waiting for Mr Rashed to turn up.

Rashed materialized out of nowhere. He smiled and, without bothering to shake hands, pulled out a chair and sat opposite me. He ordered tea.

"Nice day, is it not, Mr Hutton? Not too humid today." The petty talk of diplomacy could be a match for the circuitous conversations of the orient. We embarked on a lengthy debate about the weather, global warming, temperature records and a comparison between hot places on the planet. We eventually concurred that the French Côte d'Azur had a number of merits unparalleled anywhere in the world. He seemed determined not to start any meaningful dialogue, and I was equally determined not to show any annoyance. Having exhausted our respective knowledge of geography and travel, we drifted into the matter of the cost of living, followed by a comparative study of Dubai's fashionable restaurants. Then we discussed leisure and sports. At last he mentioned polo. He had seen a game, not long ago, and he remembered spotting me amongst the players. Quite naturally we started talking about the other team members.

"How well do you know Naji, Mr Hutton?" he asked. I felt the petty talk was suddenly over. This wasn't social chit chat anymore.

"We play polo together," I said, "and occasionally do business. You know how it is."

"Not really," he replied. "I'm a civil servant and, although my family has several businesses, I myself have no time for them and their activities. Perhaps you could enlighten me a little in a matter that has affected our common friend Mr Naji."

I felt a sudden chill in the air. "Why sure, with pleasure. Naji knows me well and he could have called me, you know." I said. But there was no way to discourage this conscientious civil servant.

He went on: "Mr Naji has recently invested a sizeable sum of money in the procurement of machinery for the manufacture of construction materials. Insulated panels or whatever. The machinery has just arrived and Customs have inspected several of the containers. The Customs manager at Jebel Ali Port is a relative of Naji, so he called him to report some astonishing findings. Naji has sent one of his staff to the Port to verify the findings of the Customs inspectors."

Rashed paused, his unwavering gaze fixed on me. I had to ask: "And what were the findings, Mr Rashed? Anything in particular? Any illegal cargo?"

"Not really. No. But most of the goods are made of rusty metal scrap. Hardly any recognizable pieces of equipment," he said.

"My God!" I exclaimed. "I'm Naji's partner in this venture. Are you sure? It cannot be. We had the goods inspected and certified in Germany!" I had a recollection of the severe-looking inspector and of the brief examination performed by our team in Hamburg. Surely this couldn't be the case. Vanhoof had organized a team and lifting equipment for the inspection to be thorough, and the serious-looking guy had taken three days to examine every single container.

"There must be mistake, Mr Rashed. Have Customs examined the right containers?" I said, clutching at already improbable straws.

"The Customs officers know their job, Mr Hutton. Since you told me you're a partner in this transaction, perhaps you can help me in investigating the origin of the upset. How do you think this could have happened? Can you give me the history of the deal from the beginning?"

I didn't like the word "investigating". And the film of the deal had too many flashbacks with Katherina in charge of developments. I felt uneasy and started worrying that I had been manipulated. To what end? If the consignment was worthless, then on the face of it, I was losing one million dollars — not mine, but nevertheless it would look like it.

I painfully and prudently began telling the story, beginning with the approach from Mr Vanhoof through the commercial network which supports the activities of the commercial attachés of the world. Then I went on to explain my personal interest as I had become a firm believer in the economic plans of the country and a staunch supporter of its policies. I had therefore decided to share with Naji in the investment opportunity afforded by Mr Vanhoof's offer. Rashed stopped me here.

"What percentage share of the opportunity have you subscribed, Mr Hutton?"

"Twenty percent," I said.

That wasn't enough to shake him off that track: "Did you invest your own money in this venture or did you act, in whole or in part, as a proxy for other business people?" he probed.

I shifted in my chair, as if to cushion a blow expected to land any moment. My friend Mr Rashed would have easy access to bank records, accounts and transactions. Banking secrecy in this country wasn't for the law. I admitted: "I put some of my money together with a contribution from a Russian investor."

"No harm in that, Mr Hutton." His encouraging smile made me more apprehensive of his motives. "And then how did you assess the feasibility — if that is the word — of the intended investment?"

Now this was a chance to divert attention. I replied, "Due diligence is a routine practice implemented by prudent investors. It includes checking the facts, the market, exploring the options, best and worst scenario and break-even point, all of which are then subjected to a risk analysis.

"Naji knows very well all the steps taken to ensure that this was a sound proposal. Amongst other precautions, we appointed a qualified engineer to review the business plan. His name is Jon and he works in a reputable local company. As for the plant itself, an inspection agency surveyed it thoroughly before shipment and issued a certified report. I will fax you the details of the agency and a copy of their report. The purchase was an attractive proposition and all safety measures were in place to make a success of it. As for the engineer who reviewed and confirmed the business plan, here are his contacts." I pulled out a pen and scribbled Jon's mobile number on a napkin.

Rashed watched me without moving. I regained my composure: calm breath, straight back, feet under the chair and unblinking gaze.

"So you're convinced there has been no attempt to, shall we say, deceive Mr Naji? You see, in our country, we're protective of our people and we like to ensure that no undue advantage is taken of their trust or ignorance. I shall welcome your assistance and goodwill in the inquiry." With that he stood up, again not bothering to shake hands, and disappeared into the milling crowd.

I waved at the waiter and asked for the bill, then called Mr Vanhoof for an explanation. His phone rang but he didn't answer. A weird feeling of impending disaster grew in my guts.

And by now it was too late to call my new-found, not-so-virtuous friend.

7. The Fall Guy

Katherina

As usual I was taking delight in the feel of Charity's young, warm body curling against my side. However, the phone broke the coziness of the moment. For Geoffrey to call me again, after the fracas at his party, there had to be serious reason. I patted the girl on the rump and pushed her out of bed. She disappeared towards the bathroom.

"Hello, Geoffrey! How are you?" No point musing over our last meeting in any way. Geoffrey was equal to the situation.

"I'm fine. What about you, Katherina?" With that we started as if nothing had happened and we forgot that he had tried to rape me. I invited him to talk.

"I had a strange meeting, Katherina. A Mr Rashed. I'm not too sure what his position may be, but he looks like police or some security branch. He told me that the plant is not really a plant and that the containers are full of rubbish. I tried to call Vanhoof, but without success. Do you have any idea about this? Have you been in touch with Vanhoof?"

Well, I had an idea indeed. Even more than an idea. The delivery of the plant had gone according to plan, but I hardly could tell him that. And dear Geoffrey had very little chance of ever talking to Mr Vanhoof again. But of course I couldn't tell him that either.

"Dear God, Geoffrey! How is this possible? I thought you knew Mr Vanhoof very well and that this deal was as solid as rock!" I said.

"Katherina! It was you yourself who told me the deal was good, right from the start. You said that Boris had Vanhoof checked out by his own contacts in Germany, that Boris had so much confidence in the business that he would put a million dollars into it. What shall I tell Boris now? That I was wrong to believe you? Please do something."

Geoffrey was raving.

He would just be a growing nuisance. We needed a fall guy here. Geoffrey had been earmarked as the perfect scapegoat: notoriously gullible, an undiscerning womanizer and amateur wheeler-dealer. I had to keep him quiet until disposal, though.

"Take it easy, please," I said reassuringly. "In the first place, the plant may be perfectly operational and just badly inspected, or inspected by people who do not have a clue about its use and operation. Let me talk to Boris. I will check at the Port as well, where I can use some of Boris's contacts. I will call you back in a day or two. In the meantime, don't worry. After all, you're not the one whose investment is at risk." With that, I put the phone down and started thinking about the next and final phase of our little scheme.

Jon

Geoffrey called in a panic. Customs had inspected the containers and found them full of scrap. Perhaps even crap from what he said. Geoffrey ended up accusing me of being the engineer of the disaster. It looked like a swindle to me and I remembered the self-conscious representative of the certifying agency: a good actor, that one. But also I couldn't allow Geoffrey to dump the responsibility of this one on me. All I had done was check business projections against market data, and then play escort to Naji and others in what proved to be a cosmetic, meaningless exercise. I also remembered with what skill Mr Vanhoof had been wasting our time in Hamburg on account of friendliness and hospitality.

"Please, Geoffrey, leave me out of this, will you? I checked your feasibility and I saw the same containers as you in Hamburg. I didn't write the business plan, or the purchase agreement, or the inspection contract. Please talk to whoever arranged those, not me please. See you some time."

With that I put the phone down. What was going on here?

8. Confrontation

Naji

I had been conned, properly and thoroughly screwed. I couldn't believe it. The thorough survey of the containers at Dubai Port had shown a commercial value of the machinery of about half a million dollars, hardly better than scrap metal. One could call it the residual value, although I didn't feel much better appreciating the pun.

I went over the individuals who had engineered the swindle.

First of all, the sleek Mr Vanhoof. He was the perfect conman — silky, charming, convincing, and then so skillful at disguising the truth and conjuring visions to replace reality. I had talked to Rashed and I was confident he would get whatever cooperation was necessary from Interpol to catch the thief.

Then there was my partner Geoffrey Hutton IV. That he was a wheeler-dealer and made use of his diplomatic status was common knowledge. So what? There was no harm in that; everybody takes advantage of what he can. That he was also a womanizer was neither here nor there. Most men are, including myself. Was Geoffrey an active or dormant accomplice of the smooth Mr Vanhoof? He had been very pushy. His million-dollar contribution may have been bait. Everything was possible.

Talking about womanizing, I should check how much Katherina was involved in the scheme with him. She was suspiciously helpful throughout. Was she an accomplice?

And Jon. I had trusted the young Irishman more than any other party to this deal. Now he too was eluding my calls. Was he possibly a part of the swindle? What was enticing enough for him in this deal to make him fly to Hamburg with our lot?

Meeting face-to-face was the only way to make sense of people. I decided to start with Jon as he was the one I distrusted the least.

It wasn't the done thing for a local businessman of my standing to go and visit an engineering employee of a foreign company. Yet Jon had avoided my calls and getting his feedback was worth a small breach of protocol. I stood up and walked past my PA's desk, telling her I would be out for an hour. As I reached the door, Katherina walked in. Talk of the devil.

I had always been intrigued by the woman. There was something sultry about her that made her a target of men's attention anywhere, anytime. Just a little too skinny for my taste. Never mind. Business first.

And she wanted to talk business. Actually she talked about the plant: "Naji, I'm so happy to see you. I was sorry to hear that the shipment has a problem. What is going on? Can you tell me?"

Where had she heard about problems? I didn't have to wait. She continued: "Our friend Geoffrey is in a state of panic, Naji. Someone met him, from Customs, or from the police, to say that the cargo was largely made of scrap steel. Are you aware of that?"

"The containers are full of scrap metal. Worthless," I said. "It seems that someone along the line has been clever. Did you know Mr Vanhoof well?"

"I didn't know him at all," she replied quickly. "I got involved at a late stage only. Geoffrey had the contact, not me. Geoffrey asked for my help in getting a verification of the feasibility, and then getting top-up funding for his share of the business. Do you think Mr Vanhoof was a crook?"

"That would be for the police to say. However, for sure things like this don't happen by accident. Whose doing could it be? Tell me! I bought the plant on Vanhoof's assurance that he had seen it working, had seen it being dismantled and had seen it being packed. I don't think he was deceived at any stage, so he must have lied. The police and Interpol will be able to tell me soon if I'm right."

I was getting carried away, but four million dollars are four million dollars.

Katherina remained composed, sounding genuine and truthful. She went on: "Sure, Vanhoof must have had a hand in it then. But do you think he was alone?"

She had a point and her thought was connecting with mine. "Who knows? What would you say?"

She thought for a while. "Jon gave you a report which encouraged you to buy the plant. He could have done it on purpose... I would give him the benefit of the doubt, though." She paused, and then without a prompt, dropped a stunner "You know, Geoffrey was so persuasive on this deal. I often wondered what interest he had in insulating panels. He had no previous experience in that industry, no knowledge at all. Anyway, he's a friend and we shouldn't have unsupported, perhaps unjustified reservations about him."

Despite the backpedalling at the end of that statement, Katherina had been leaning heavily on her so-called friend. Did she know more?

From then on, our conversation remained unproductive.

*

Jon wasn't surprised to see me. I invited him for a drive and we left in my Bentley.

"I was worried about you," I said. "I called you a couple of times. Did you not notice my calls?"

"Sorry," replied Jon. "Life has been very hectic over the past few days. You know, I'm just a paid man and I owe allegiance to the company. They tend to take advantage at times."

I had been uncharacteristically direct, and he had been uncharacteristically blunt in his indirect jibe. I changed tack. "Listen, Jon. There is no doubt by now that the deal has been a big scam. I have lost four million US and I'm not happy about it. You encouraged me to make the deal. You have a responsibility in this situation."

"Please!" he exclaimed. "All I did was cross-check a feasibility study. The figures made sense and I said so. What you made of that verification was your choice. And the feasibility study together with the check were based on a real plant. You should talk to Mr Vanhoof. He has to do the explaining."

Still I probed: "What do you think of Geoffrey's participation in the deal? It didn't occur to me before, but how did the business come to him in the first place? He's not in that line. Do you have any idea?"

Jon was fretting. "Geoffrey's job is full of business opportunities, by default. His very job is to create business opportunities! But please, Naji, I don't want to speculate about other people. Why don't you talk to Geoffrey? I'm sure he will tell you all you want to know."

Saying too little, as Jon was doing, could be as damning as saying too much, as Katherina had done. I felt more and more suspicious of our friend Geoffrey.

I dropped Jon back at his office and picked up my mobile. I had a good friend, an ex-school mate, in the Ministry of Foreign Affairs in Abu Dhabi. He would know how to treat a fishy diplomat.

9. The End

Jon

The Blue Note was crowded — loud Westerners drinking beer at the bar, small groups of Asians clustered around tables, waiters going back and forth with trays high in the air. I found a table in a corner and settled down with a tall glass of ice-cold lager, the very look of which was already refreshing.

I mused about the possible rescue plans and discarded one after the other.

Geoffrey arrived half an hour late. He wasn't the Geoffrey of old, dynamic, proactive and on-the-dot. He looked disheveled, walking at a slow pace and not throwing a single glance at any of the pretty girls sitting in the lounge. He pulled up a chair and sat down. When the waiter asked for his order he couldn't make up his mind and eventually settled for a coffee after a long, hesitant review of the menu.

"Nice to see you, Jon," he started. "This will probably be my farewell. The Ministry has assigned me to the embassy in Khartoum. I should be going next week. What do you say?"

I was startled. Geoffrey was almost an institution in the city: charming, articulate, genial, or wanting to be all that. And now this wrecked, depressed man? Obviously the assignment in the Sudanese capital was no advancement to his career. Although I found some traits of his character less than appealing, I still had some friendship for the man. After all we had played polo together, we had dined and wined, and we shared a couple of views and interests. I tried to be positive: "Hey, Khartoum? That place can only go up, and you will be at the heart of a big expansion. For sure you will have lots of opportunities. Have you been there before? Do they have polo or golf in Khartoum?"

He remained gloomy, as you would expect. "Khartoum is a dump, and there will be no growth or expansion as long as there is no peace settlement in Darfur. I have been demoted, Jon. I'm pissed off. After all my efforts and successes here. What do they know of my ability at the Ministry? Is that all I get in recognition of what I achieved here?" He took a sip of his coffee.

"Don't worry, Geoffrey. You will find ways to show your capabilities again. And by the way I'm told that Sudanese women can be extremely beautiful. You will miss Katherina, though," I said, hoping that my taunt would cheer him up a little.

It certainly got Geoffrey's attention. "Don't mention that bitch," he exclaimed. "Do you know she's a man?"

I felt like I'd blush. As a matter of fact, I'd felt more than fondness towards Katherina. And to realize that my penchant had been directed at a man... My mother—God bless her—would be horrified that her son's careful and loving education had resulted in such a deviant inclination. I couldn't resist asking: "Really? How did you find out?"

He shrugged. "What do you think? The hard way," he said.

I was prudent enough not to ask for further details.

EUROPE

THE CEMETERY

OF THE ELEPHANTS

*When old elephants feel their end is near,
they disappear in the savannah, never to be seen again.*
African legend

As soon as he started the uphill walk he realized he was too fast again, a habit he had not been able to control despite years on the slopes. There was no hurry though. There never was, and definitely not this time. He slowed down and forced himself into a slow pace. Even so he was short of breath after a few steps.

The path meandered through pine trees. The soil, still gorged by the rain, gave off the rich smell of humus. Patches of sun had found their way through the tree cover, warming up the shoulders of the old man.

As always he resisted the temptation to look back and measure the ground already covered. He knew he would be disappointed. He had hardly passed the first bend in the path when his panting became more than he could sustain. As always, he gave himself the excuse of looking at the scenery to catch up his breath. He could see the other side of the valley through the branches: the light green of the grass, the grey rocks, the blue sky and the white, white, lonely clouds. Birds were singing. His heart rejoiced briefly as his breathing returned to normal. The pain in his chest was still there, though, ebbing back and forth with a life of its own. Funny to say that this portent of death had a life. He had a tired smile at his wit. He started walking again, maintaining a slower pace.

It took him an hour to get through the pine forest. He stopped only four times to catch his breath and rest his aching legs, which he considered a success. The place he wanted to reach was now visible. Above the grassy slope, rocky outcrops looked like the towers of a timeless citadel. There was a crag up there, with a crevice facing the sun. That was the place. Another hour to go.

Out of the shade of the trees, the sun was stronger and he discarded his windbreaker; he would not need it from now on. He drank the rest of the water and, still conscious of the unspoilt mountain, wrapped the empty plastic bottle in the abandoned garment. From above the tree line, the eye could catch the distant ranges, some still capped in snow. He felt his soul breathing, much better than his chest. He moved again, careful to be slow and save the last sparkles of his energy. The pain ebbed forth and he waited a minute to let it pass. He considered sitting down but fought back the temptation. He may not have been able to stand up again. He put a foot forward, and then the next. And again.

There was perspiration on his forehead, the drops unhurriedly following the wrinkles of his face. The slope was steeper now and the puffing got out of hand. He stopped, his legs trembling under him, his head spinning. He sat down, facing the sun. A red veil descended on his closed eyes. The world shrank into the bright screen of his eyelids, the warmth of the afternoon sun on his drying face, the unrelenting pain and the approaching peace. His mind drifted back to the crack in the rocks, up there, tranquil and peaceful, waiting for his body. He resisted the appeal of lying down: here or there were not the same thing. The choice was there, not here, on this empty slope.

From his sitting position, he turned to one side, half kneeling, trying to stand again. The pain was now blinding him, a grey veil cancelling all other sensations. He made a last effort, his confused mind jumbling old beliefs. Tough guys don't dance. Nor do they cry. Nor do they give up.

Still on his knees, he placed his hands flat on the ground. The pain reached a new level. A bright flash in his eyes obliterated any remaining determination, and his body rolled in the soft grass.

133

Naphthalene
Must Be Banned

"My God! My God! Why have you forsaken me?"

I knew my end was near. The pain in my lungs was excruciating and the spasms didn't stop, no matter what. I could hardly move a limb now. Our daughter, the younger and weaker of our children, had passed away the day before and collapsed in the abyss below our settlement. Now I would touch the face of my wife: she would not move, the contractions in her chest were the only remaining signs of life. She was going to die very soon. As for the boy, his young vitality had only extended his agony. He was looking at me with unspeakable despair in his trusting eyes. I hoped he would not survive me.

Our small family, or what was left of it, was the last remnant of a once-prosperous community. Not so long ago, the air was clean, food was plentiful, and social life pleasant. Children were happy. We educated them in the traditional ways with the confidence that their life and that of their own children would perpetuate the culture and habits of our race.

And then, one cursed day, an anonymous criminal hand left the abominable, pestilential balls in our midst. At first we didn't pay much attention. There was an odd smell, not particularly offensive, so we carried on with our daily chores: gathering food, educating the kids. After a couple of days, though, the elderly started coughing. The breathing discomfort quickly affected everybody, and the old folks soon became seriously ill. A particularly astute and observant neighbor associated the plague with the balls which appeared to release a steady stream of noxious gases. Already many of us were weak from the inhalation of the poisonous fumes. The neighbor had a point. The stronger and healthier of our lot put their shoulders to the monstrous spheres and attempted to roll them forward towards the cliff. If only we had a bit more strength! They pushed till the strain in their limbs reached breaking point. The balls didn't move. They mobilized their last ounce of energy, took a deep lethal breath and heaved with all their soul. The curse didn't move. Exhausted and helpless, our people collapsed.

Prayer was then the only recourse. With all our weakening hearts, we implored God to have mercy on us. Surely we're all equal in His creation. Is the suffering of a toad less worthy than the hurt of a lion, does the emotion of a primate rate above the passion of a cockroach? Even a plant may display a grief which merits attention: the azalea on the window sill wrinkles its foliage when its attendant forgets to water the pot. We beg you, Lord! Do not abandon your children!

But the darkness remained silent. Are we a condemned species? Why us?

Surely in some other life, on some other planet, mothballs will be banned.

HARD LUCK

The man was driving the convertible at a leisurely pace. The light wind ruffled his dark curly hair. In the open shirt a gold medallion shone against the tan of his chest. He drummed on the wheel with his fingers, in tune with a blues from the sound system. There was a bag on the passenger seat, of the type known as a "baise-en-ville" by his countrymen.

The sign said: "Aosta 110km". The road wound through back country, in a landscape of olive trees and dry grass. The air smelled of lavender. The dark blue of the Mediterranean would appear in the rear view mirror every once in a while, as the road swerved around the hills. There was a contented smile on the driver's face.

He caught the billboard from the corner of his eye and hit the brakes hard. He reversed the car a few meters to read it again. There was no mistaking. The board said "Convento di Suore di San Donato Milanese—Prostituzione". His air of contentment gave way to perplexity. Then a bigger smile stretched the creases of his face. Wasn't the "position du missionaire" best suited to a nun? He put the car back into gear and turned in the direction indicated by the board.

He was now changing gear and handling the wheel with a sense of purpose. No more drumming. He drove faster. Something big was coming up.

The convent came into view as the road entered a small valley. The building, worthy of Palladio, had the stateliness befitting the Church, with a tranquil serenity matching the countryside. Cypress trees gave shade to a car park stretching along the main facade. The driver stopped the car near the portal, walked to the gate, pulled the cord of the brass bell and waited, shifting his weight from one leg to the other.

At last a sister opened the heavy door. She had a comely face and a hint of blonde hair under the head scarf. The grey robe was slit at the side, Far East style. He caught a glimpse of white flesh above a black stocking.

"Welcome," she said. "That will be one hundred euros, please. Do you want a receipt?"

"No need, thanks," he said, handing her the money.

The nun made an entry in a register, closed it with a flurry, placed the money in a drawer and pointed to a corridor: "That way, please. Just follow the signs."

The man started at a brisk pace. Soon though his thoughts caused him to slow down. The corridor had a couple of turns but the arrows kept pointing so he went on. He came to a large solid wooden door with a sign saying "Enter here". He entered without hesitation.

The door opened on to the far corner of the car park. A large board under a cypress tree said "Dear visitor, in conformity with your wish, you have been screwed by the sisters of San Donato. We thank you for your donation. Have a good day. Drive carefully".

The man paused for a while, then walked back to his car. There was something limp in his gait.

THE MEETING

The ground, still cool from the morning dew, was releasing the freshness of the night. The sun, however, already high in the blue spring sky, was lusciously warm on the shoulders of the deer. The animals were immobile, standing in the sparkling grass, watching the cars hurrying towards Richmond Gate.

In the secluded surroundings of Isabella Garden, the beasts of the forest started their daily chores: a woodpecker was heartily hammering a dead twig on a large oak tree, a hedgehog scurried towards its favorite diner and doves cooed in the high branches.

Reassured by the familiar sounds of the garden, the rabbit stepped out of his burrow and stretched on the narrow path. He smelled the water of the pond on his right. He was thirsty and started moving contentedly, the sun warm on his back and the rich scent of the forest in his nostrils. The surface of the path was springy under his paws. The rabbit was happy, blind, but happy. Naturally he depended on sound and smell for guidance, but he had developed his senses to a high degree. He was secure and comfortable in his environment.

So it was a serious shock to his system when he stumbled on a completely unannounced obstacle standing in the middle of the well-trodden way to the pond. The crash had been soft and he had felt the consistency of soft flesh in the mild collision.

"I'm sorry," said the rabbit "My eyesight is poor and I didn't see you."

A gentle, feminine voice answered, "Not to worry, love. It happens to me all the time."

"Still, my apologies," said the rabbit, "but pray tell me how is it you're prone to accidents all the time?"

The gentle voice responded again: "I'm blind, you see. So when I park myself in the wrong place, I'm bound to be hit, especially by quiet people. But who are you to be so kind and yet suffer from the same condition?"

By then the rabbit was enthralled: a feminine encounter, a shared frailty, a magic morning. "Would you want to guess?" said he.

"With pleasure," said the frog (for a frog it was). "But may I have some clues? May I touch you?"

The plot in the rabbit's mind was developing better and better. You know how rabbits are. "With pleasure," he said with a slight swagger of the hips, obviously unseen by the frog. So the frog proceeded: "I can feel soft fur, long ears, a bob of a tail. You must be a rabbit!" she exclaimed.

"Right!" said the delighted rabbit, anticipating the return courtesy. "And may I now guess who you are?" he asked, full of hope.

"Sure," the frog replied. "And if you promise to behave, you may touch me as well."

"Promise, promise," uttered the rabbit in a hurry and, without further ado, he proceeded to palm the owner of the lovely voice.

"Let me see. Short legs? Protruding eyes? Slimy skin? What is your nationality?"

DINNER

A faint smell of cigars mixed with the heady scent of natural flowers on the tables. Waiters were gliding noiselessly on the thick carpet. Except for the soft yellow shades on the occupied tables, the restaurant was dark. Classical music, barely audible, underlay the hum of conversation. The velvety setting made for an atmosphere of relaxed, distinguished wellbeing.

They walked in. He, tall, grey hair parted and combed close to the skull, three-piece suit in a twenty-year-old cut, club tie. She, hair tied in an austere bun, lips tight, a necklace with a single strand of small pearls on her pale skin, a straight ankle-long grey dress, flat shoes.

The maitre d' met them: "Good evening Mr Smith, Mrs Smith." He led them to the table which had been theirs for ages past. They sat face to face, but they had turned their backs to each other long ago.

"Camparis as usual?" asked the maitre d', handing out menus. They nodded and flipped through the pages. She closed the menu and waited for him to make up his mind. The Camparis arrived, placed with ceremony by a solemn waiter. They ordered. He, asparagus with a white sauce, followed by grilled cod. She, artichoke, and then liver with gratin and vegetables. She said, "You may order the same Sancerre we had last time." He dutifully arranged the wine, insisting on the correct temperature and an ice bucket in an unexpected outburst of rhetoric.

They ate in silence. They didn't avoid looking at each other. It is just that they didn't see each other anymore. The asparagus and artichokes came and went. They tapped their lips with the napkins in unconscious unison. He motioned for a waiter to refill their glasses. There was a lull ahead of the main dishes being served. They both assessed the neighboring diners. They did not discuss their impressions.

She found the liver undercooked and got him to send it back to the kitchen. The maitre d' apologized profusely. She said to no-one in particular, "Service is no longer what it used to be." He nodded prudently. The liver came back after a while.

Before the dessert she went to the powder room. She returned with a shade of pink on her high cheeks. He stood up to advance her chair. They resumed their sphinx-like posture. She said, "This time I will have crème brûlée." He signaled a waiter and ordered the crème brûlée and a custard. They skipped coffee and liqueurs. He settled in cash, pulling banknotes from a thin, worn out wallet. She impatiently fidgeted with her bag, ready to go, whilst he was still counting the change.

They left without a word, nodding at the maitre d' as they passed him, walking side by side, so far apart.

THE SHAFT

1

The boy had been exploring this new territory for some time. The recently-discovered forest was outside the familiar playground near his home.

Nearer his parents' house, in the fields and copses, he had played hide-and-seek, a companion of Robin Hood. There he knew every tree and every rock, every path and every trail. In one particular cluster of pine trees a large plant of climbing clematis had left a screen of hanging lianas from which he could swing across space like the lord of the jungle. He knew where rabbits used to play and where pheasants would hatch. He had conquered Jerusalem, standing on battlements made of a derelict lime kiln lost in a cove. In a sloping pasture, he had battled screaming Sioux warriors alongside William Custer. He was the master of an invisible realm.

That late afternoon he accompanied Henri Morton Stanley in a distant exploration. The trek took them to the other side of the road which marked the boundary of his empire, but he couldn't turn down Mr Stanley's invitation. They hiked through the underbrush, going uphill. Soon he was alone, he had lost Mr Stanley somewhere in his history books. He continued on his own; a true explorer is not put off by loneliness. The ascent was endless. He puffed heavily, but by now the challenge had taken on momentous proportions. He had to know what was at the top. He had a fleeting concern about his mother, who had little interest in the discovery of Africa and no tolerance for late boys. Still, the top couldn't be far. He pressed on through the unfamiliar jungle.

And on he went. Sure enough, there was an end to the gradient. The edge of the forest was lined with a fence made of tight strands of barbed wire. A large grazing pasture covered the plateau in all directions. In the middle, in front of his avid eyes, was a copse, a hundred yards away, maybe a hundred yards in size. The perfect fortress: a clear line of fire all around, impenetrable cover, in the heart of Africa. The boy crawled under the barbed wire and moved with caution, in case the fortress was occupied by hostile forces, or in case the farmer owning the pasture would object.

Contrary to his fears, the crossing was uneventful. He reached another fence of barbed wire encircling the thicket. He squeezed underneath the wire and, bending over, made his way through the thick undergrowth. He covered hardly twenty feet and the bushes disappeared. There was a huge hole in the ground, in the shape of a funnel, some hundred feet in diameter. The face of the conical opening was covered in unstable rubble. In the centre of the funnel, forty feet below, was the dark mouth of a shaft disappearing into the entrails of the earth. The boy's heart missed several beats. He stepped cautiously on the slope and immediately a small landslide of debris slithered a few feet towards the gaping orifice.

The boy stepped back and ran half the way back home to avoid the wrath of his mother. His heart was somersaulting, not only because of the running.

2

Ever since his discovery of the pit, the boy dreamt about it: was there a treasure hidden there? A secret palace? An underground battle station? He had to go there. But there may be danger. He needed help. There is security in numbers. On the other hand, he was jealous of his discovery; it wasn't to be shared with the bullies of the village, for sure.

The answer struck him on the third day. Dirk and Ollie, his Dutch friends, foreigners on holiday and due to leave in a couple of weeks. Occasional playmates. Cool guys. They didn't speak the lingua but so what? The boy knew a few words of Flemish and professionals can easily understand each other by gestures and other means.

He told them of the expedition in the forest beyond the road and the discovery of a mysterious shaft plunging deep underground. Dutch people have little inclination towards daydreaming and fantasies. Dirk, the elder of the two, a sturdy adolescent of 14 years of age, surmised that the shaft may be the access to an ancient subterranean quarry. Ollie, Dirk's lanky younger brother, concurred. He would always agree with Dirk, no matter what the subject. Still, the prosaic explanation would not deter the boy from his burning desire to investigate the cavernous opening, nor would it stop the receivers of the boy's secret exploring the mysterious hole. The three of them agreed to investigate the site.

They left early to have ample time at the site. The crossing of the forest and the meadow were uneventful. They sneaked under the last barbed wire fence and stole through the bushes. The abyss was there, waiting.

The boys circled the rim of the funnel. From the opposite they saw the tip of a rusting ladder anchored on the wall of the rectangular opening at the bottom of the scree cone. The scree-covered slope, however, was slippery on all sides. Dirk tested it with his foot and then with some heavy stones thrown in: the scree was at the limit of stability and any additional weight carelessly placed on the incline would cause a mini-avalanche. The boys threw pebbles in the shaft mouth gaping at the bottom of the funnel. They heard the echo of the stones bouncing against the walls of the shaft.

The boys held a war council. The scree was off-putting but the enticement of the ladder was irresistible. Dirk again took the lead. He cautiously rolled over the rim and lay, spread-eagled, on the slope. The unstable rubble didn't shift. He then unhurriedly shifted one limb at a time. Slowly he descended within the funnel, towards the tip of the ladder. He progressed at an agonizingly slow pace. The boy and Ollie, watching from the top, bit their nails, fearing that Dirk would trigger a landslide and disappear into the gaping hole.

He made it to the edge of the shaft and the top of the ladder in about three minutes and shouted a report in Dutch. The boy understood from this that the shaft was going down. Big deal! He shouted questions back. He couldn't make any sense from the replies. Well, if Dirk had done it, so could he. He stretched over the rim and lay down on the slope. Then in imitation of Dirk's performance, he started creeping down, his heart in his mouth, his senses alert to the slightest tremor in the stones under his body. Within two minutes, he was next to Dirk, peering down at the shaft and the ladder.

The well was rectangular in shape, about twenty feet by thirty, slightly off the vertical and plunging into darkness at a very steep angle. The ladder was near a corner, anchored to the rock. The iron was heavily corroded by rust but the ladder appeared to be in workable condition. The two boys gazed down. The ladder disappeared into the gloom. They gazed at each other.

The boy placed a hand on Dirk's shoulder. "I will do it this time," he said. Still lying flat on the rubble, he carefully rotated his body until his legs were pointing down. He shifted his weight to the rungs and grabbed the side of the ladder. The fourth rung gave way under the load. His heart jumped. He went back up, his knuckles white on the metal. He peered down. The bent rung was particularly corroded, the others less so. He went down again, stepping over the faulty tread, his knuckles still white. He was shivering from the strain. Slowly, carefully, he climbed down about thirty feet. His eyesight adjusted to the gloom and he could make out the shape of the shaft. He could actually see the bottom, another hundred feet below. His heart missed a beat: the ladder stopped fifty feet short of it.

The rectangular shaft being off the vertical, the face opposite the ladder made a steeply inclined roof over the boy's head. An icy drop of water fell on his head, causing his heart to miss several more beats. Clinging to the sides of the ladder, he climbed back up, his hands rigid on the sides of the ladder. He stepped over the rusted rung and crawled flat next to the waiting Dirk. He was out breath.

They both crawled carefully back out of the scree cone and held a pow-wow, Ollie listening intently.

3

The boy rummaged in the loft. He was sure that long ago he had seen a manila rope. He removed old canteens and cardboard suitcases. He pushed aside piles of ancient magazines. There it was, under a derelict armchair that had spilled its stuffing. A large coil of rope, three quarters of an inch in diameter. He grabbed the end and gave it a pull between his two hands: He found the test conclusive and placed the coil on his shoulder.

Dirk was duly impressed. So was Ollie. Between them, in addition to the rope, the boys gathered two electric torches, one pocket knife and a large fisherman's blade in a sheath. They found the preparations satisfactory and decided to make their move the next day.

By now the walk across the road, through the forest and into the meadow was routine. There was no farmer in sight. The three lads entered the thicket and gathered at the point of the rim from where they could descend straight to the iron ladder. Having contributed the rope the boy claimed precedence and, the rope coiled on his shoulder, he made his way down, slowly, slowly. Having practiced the descent and climb once before gave him the confidence that comes from familiarity. Without a pause that could have weakened his resolve, he stepped on the ladder and, avoiding the fourth rung, he started the descent.

He passed the point that he had reached on the previous exploration. The air was distinctly colder. The rock face, a few inches in front of him, shone with moisture and slime. On the positive side, the ladder was in good shape. He did slow down though, looking down to figure out the next moves. He could now make out the bottom of the pit, full of rubble, and a couple of discarded wooden joists. In the face of the wall opposite the ladder, he could discern the dark entrance of a tunnel.

Dirk had started descending above him. There was no way to turn around now. He went down and down, his knuckles white on the side of the ladder. As he reached the bottom step, he released one end of the manila rope from the coil and looped it around several rungs, tying it with multiple knots on to a solid-looking rung. Then he let go of the rope. The coil undid itself and the excess length of the rope fell in a heap at the bottom of the pit.

Now Ollie too was on the way down. Dirk arrived and pointed out that the rope length might be sufficient to double it up. The boy caught the idea and pulled back the entire length till he had the other end in his hand. Then, holding the lose end tight in his fist, he let go of the loop and to their delight, they found that the length of the rope was just double the depth from the end of the ladder to the bottom of the pit. He tied the second end of the rope in like fashion to a solid-looking rung, gave it a pull and then looked at Dirk.

Dirk was about ten feet above him. To give Dirk the privilege of being the first to rappel down would have meant a precarious switch of position. Having claimed the seniority in the team with the contribution of the rope, the boy was stuck. He cursed his recklessness and, grabbing the two strands together in his hands, he left the safety of the ladder. Going down was easier than he expected and he landed on the floor with a relief in his muscles and in his mind. He had hardly gathered his wits when Dirk arrived and then Ollie. They didn't talk but looked at each other with a solemnity beyond their age.

They turned towards the dark gallery, switched on their two torches and walked in the passageway. The tunnel was wide and high enough for all three to walk in line abreast. The ground was even and clean. It still had the sleepers of a narrow-gage railway. They went hardly fifty yards and came to a cliff, on the edge of a cavernous space. Their feeble lights couldn't pierce the darkness to the ends of the cave. There was no visible hold and no way to climb down into the huge grotto. They went back to the base of the pit and, crestfallen, had a look at the loop of their rope hanging from the ladder.

4

They toured the bottom of the shaft, a task taking all of one minute. They walked down the gallery again, still with no option other than to come back. There was only one thing to do: go back up and out.

The boy had the first go. The fact that the shaft wasn't exactly vertical was both a blessing and a curse. The steep rock face gave something to lean against, but it was somehow in the way as well. He couldn't climb as if the rope was hanging free. The rope, by then, had sustained the weight of three descents. The traction had both elongated the fibers and thinned the line. Furthermore, the rope had rubbed against the muddy face of the rock and had become as slippery as an eel. There was no grip. The boy went up about ten feet and fell back. Dirk pushed him aside and had a go. He went up twenty feet and gave up.

Ollie, who carried the fisherman's blade, tried to cut a makeshift ladder or scaffold out of the forgotten wooden joists. He managed to gouge his hand before achieving any worthwhile assembly. That incident ruled him out as a climber.

Now seriously worried the kids sat down, looking up at the cursed rope and at the damp, nearly vertical, rock face. Then the boy remembered an exercise he'd performed on his school's physical education course. There was a rope with knots every two feet, easier to climb as the knots would give support to the feet. They discussed the principle and eventually agreed to give it a try. It was a measure of the boy's fright and despair that he agreed to cut the rope in two, at the middle of the hanging loop in order to have two free strands where knots could be tied. The plan was simple: make knots as high as possible on one strand and then climbing on the knots thus prepared, make knots as high as possible on the other strand. Thus alternating position and knots preparation, one could gradually go up. Theoretically.

The boy started to demonstrate the method. It wasn't as easy as the theory as his weight pressed his body against the rock and impeded his movements. Nevertheless he managed fifteen or twenty feet, with great difficulty. His weight on the knots was creating such a pull that the volume of the knots had been reduced to a slight bump along the length of the ropes and hardly provided any of the expected support. He ground his teeth, determined not to give up despite his shaking legs and aching arms.

He reached twenty five feet up. The trembling was such that he had to let go or his hands and limbs would betray him on their own. To give respite to his throbbing, slipping hands, he bit the rope and actually hung a few seconds by the strength of his jaws. Of course gravity, pulling down his body, caused his mouth to twist in alignment with the upward rope. The pain was too much. He let go. His body slipped along the rock, the friction lifting his shirt and pullover. He landed in a heap with streaks of slime and blood on his chest. In a daze, he brushed the muck with the back of his hand and pulled the clothes down. He sat in a lump, too shaken to speak or do anything. From a corner of his dazed eye, he saw, without registering, that Dirk was having a go at climbing the ropes.

5

Dirk never said how he did it. He was strong, with a gritty determination. How much he suffered going up, how tempted to give up he might have been, only Dirk knows. When the boy came out of his trance, Dirk had disappeared. The ropes, wet, slimy and elongated, were hanging lifeless from the iron ladder fifty feet above. The boy tried again to climb but the fight had gone out of him. He gave up and sat next to Ollie, their minds blank and their eyes vague.

When he reached the top, Dirk got out of the thicket and into the meadow. He scanned the horizon and noticed the spire of a church in the distance. He set out towards it. The first problem he had to resolve was to find a person that would understand him: his Dutch wasn't commonly used in this French-speaking region. He assumed that the priest might have a better knowledge of the world than the local farmers. It took him half an hour to reach the church. He found it empty. He examined the houses nearby and spotted a cross engraved on a lintel. Dirk rang the bell under the cross and the priest came out. Combining the few French words at Dirk's disposal and the few Dutch words understood by the priest, the story started to emerge. Dirk went out to point the direction of the pit. The priest was aware of the ancient slate quarries. At some stage there had been thirty active pits around the village, which famously counted as many cafés as quarries. The last one had stopped its operations twenty years before. So had most of the cafés.

The priest was a pragmatic man and a thinker. He picked up his phone and called a speleology club in the nearest city. He was lucky — and so were the boys — that an understanding member picked up the phone.

Two hours later, a helmeted figure climbed down the iron ladder. A safety line secured him to the top, carefully watched by a colleague. As he reached the bottom rung of the iron ladder, the figure uncoiled a narrow rope ladder with steel wire strands. He fastened it and climbed down to the bottom of the shaft.

What he said, Ollie and the boy never remembered. Shivering, they went up, closely followed by the helmeted figure.

The boy got home three hours late. His mother told him off, though not as badly as he had feared. Perhaps his disheveled appearance and distressed expression had something to do with the leniency.

I never told my mother the details of that day.

ASIA

THE JOURNEYS OF THE BUTTERFLIES

1. The Far East, April

"Are you working with Max?"

The short Chinese girl with a round, dour face and long straight hair was holding a paper with my name. She appeared offended. "I'm Max," she said. So much for an introduction.

Max of course was an important feature of my visit to China. He or, rather improbably, she had organized my hotel bookings and without him/her I was well and truly stranded. Max Lee was the export manager of the company I was visiting in Beijing and she had kindly arranged my stopover in Guangzhou on the way. I had not expected, however, to meet him/her here and at this late hour.

So, great! I wasn't lost and the short lady, with a strong purposeful stride, took charge of my destiny. To the seasoned traveler, an airport is an airport is an airport. This one, though, was a Chinese airport and I gratefully followed her. From behind, her figure appeared more forthcoming and shapely than the stern unsmiling face had suggested. I briefly reflected upon the embarrassment of having called her Mr Lee in my earlier correspondence, concluding that I wasn't responsible for that male first name of hers. It made for intriguing thoughts, though.

Our business trip across the Far East had a tight schedule. However, I was vaguely hoping that in these faraway surroundings some adventurous and exotic encounter would spice up my dying conjugal life. Not that I had an unhappy family. Actually my wife is a great lady. A heart as big as a barn, forever cheerful, she had also been very beautiful, in the manner of Ava Gardner. With time, her excessive weight had blunted our appetite for one another, and money arguments had broken the old complicity. We now had friendly parallel existences, with little or no intrusion into each other's traffic lane. Our son, a wonderful 18-year-old guy with a cool wit and a friendly disposition, was the main anchor of our married life.

The first impression that Max gave me, with her crooked "tiger" tooth and her slightly crossed eyes in the dull Chinese face, was one of disappointment. I decided to bury my luscious dreams of oriental delight for the time being as we strolled into the darkness of the car park. Naturally my colleague and I were grateful for having been met on arrival. We dutifully proffered the thanks expected in such circumstances and we sat in the cab, me in the middle of the back seat and Max to my right. As we settled, I could see a tear on the knee of her black tights. She pulled down the hem of her dress in a prudish way and sat as erect as a well-mannered school girl. The car was small and I could feel the warmth of Max's leg against my thigh. I apologized for my earlier blunder of having called her Mister.

And then the first miracle happened. Max laughed. Her laugh was light, crystal clear and genuine. It sounded like a gentle waterfall, it suggested flowers and butterflies, and it had the wholehearted quality of a great human being. Max was used to being called Mister, and some mischievous streak of her character enjoyed the confusion. With the ice broken we embarked on light banter, mixed with the usual questions and answers of first-time visitors. Max took us for a late snack — it was well past midnight — in a typical suburban restaurant where the waitresses stood in line chuckling and giggling at my struggle with the chopsticks. Max was now having a good time, running a live commentary of my performance.

*

We stayed two days in Guangzhou. When her schedule allowed it, Max would turn up at our hotel and take charge of our life, in an easy and efficient manner. She knew our difficulties with the Chinese environment. She would skillfully and unobtrusively resolve the hundred and one snags affecting Westerners in those parts. She was also good company, her wonderful laugh refreshing our lame jokes.

By some fortuitous circumstance, every time we had to take a cab, I ended up sitting in the middle, with Max's hip pressing against mine with the occasional bumps of the ride. My colleague Abdullah, very much a ladies' man, was clearly jealous of my privileged riding position.

One evening, prompted by Abdullah, we decided to check out the karaoke bar lavishly advertised in the lobby of our hotel. By then well settled in her self-appointed role of mother hen, Max led our small group into the deep red, velvety lobby, negotiated with the mamasan and decided on our drinks. A couple of smiling girls sat with us in a private lounge and obligingly laughed at Abdullah's attempts to be the party boy. The ladies sang in turn, they sat close, they giggled, they drank tea, they smiled again. All the while, Max was translating, organizing, refreshing the drinks, chatting us up. There ensued a protracted negotiation between the uncomprehending girls and my colleague, the latter hoping to persuade the ladies to end the night in his bed. Max, as a true sales person, was heeding our every whim and helpfully translating the various points being made by the parties to the negotiation.

Max left us for the restroom. Abdullah's conversation with the tall doll with slanted eyes and large boobs came to an abrupt end. He turned to me and said, "These girls are nice, but Max is a lot more pleasant. Do you think we stand a chance with her rather than with these two ladies?"

I was taken aback. I'm not a party animal, nor do I customarily chase ladies. But Max's pervasive charm and indomitable presence had already marked me, somehow. It was also very clear, however, that Max was no karaoke girl, neither in her manners, nor in her education, nor in anything at all. I told Abdullah that in my view Max had placed herself out of bounds and making a pass at her would not be well received. Max came back and eventually the party dissolved. We went to bed alone.

*

Our journey continued to Beijing. Max took the same flight and we were now standing on the curb outside the airport, waiting for her company car to pick us up. "Where will you be going now, Max? Do you have an apartment here?" Both Abdullah and I were keen to know more about this little person, so great in many ways. We'd both developed a soft spot for her, gentle and yet strong, reserved and yet attractive, unobtrusive and yet intelligent.

Max's face became stern and unsmiling again: "What do you think? I'm going back to my husband and to my three children, of course."

The answer was like a blow to my stomach. I could see that Abdullah too was rattled. Well, what could we expect? We had arrived in China a couple of days before, met this girl out of the blue, and she being professionally polite with us had a right to expect nothing more than professional courtesy. Still we felt a distinct nostalgia at realizing that she stood on the other bank of a very wide canyon. She must have sensed our distress. "Do you really believe that?" she said. "I'm far too busy to have a family. I work all the time."

Why should I be relieved? And why should she tease us in this way? I had held my breath, and now I was alive again. I ventured some indigent remark to the effect that she being married was a perfectly credible proposition, seeing that there must have been at least five hundred million wanting candidates in the country. Max probably didn't understand my mutterings.

*

Our stay in Beijing followed the same pattern as the visit to Guangzhou: Max resumed her role of guide, mentor and mother hen, and I was fortunate enough to have another couple of taxi rides with her to my right. We had a couple of meals and drinks together. We came to know her better. Max was a bona fide mechanical engineer, specialized in pressure vessels. Her career had started in the oil and gas business. I had enough knowledge in the matter to realize that she was a thorough and competent professional.

Our banter continued, a favorite topic being our respective dates of birth. I had ventured that Max was wiser than her age, and dangerous to boot, on account of her uncanny perception. She wasn't too sure whether this was a compliment.

The visit to the Great Wall was a compulsory and windy intermission between our business meetings. We were disappointed that Max didn't accompany us, but obviously she had a career beyond caring for Abdullah and me. We met again in the evening and planned our last day in mainland China. The next morning Max would go with me to a factory in the Beijing suburbs that made steel fabrication equipment, whilst Abdullah would have a late morning and do some shopping.

That's how the second miracle happened. Perhaps I initiated it by asking why she had taunted us with that pretense at being married. Perhaps it was another inconsequential question. Perhaps she was simply despondent for some reason and needed to open up. Whatever the trigger, Max talked of her loneliness, of the difficulties with her boss, of the distance from her family, far away in kilometers and in attitudes. I said that all humans are lonely, that bosses need to be managed, and families need to be respected.

We discovered that the ways of coping with solitude, with prickly bosses and with old fashioned parents were identical the world over. We discovered that there was a similarity between her condition and whatever I had been through in my already longish life. The ride through the city was long and the nascent empathy was growing into a deepening mutual recognition to a point that I thought she might cry. Max was strong, though, and it would not have been self pity, rather relief at being acknowledged, after years of emotional self restraint. We kept silent for the rest of the trip, uneasy with too much having been meant and too little having been said.

*

Later that day, Max took us to the airport. The mystical complicity of the drive to the factory had disappeared in Abdullah's presence. There was a touch of sadness at the prospect of parting company. We had exchanged business cards, of course, and we had all scribbled mobile numbers as well as private emails to conjure separation. We promised to send each other the pictures taken during dinners and elsewhere.

The third miracle happened at the airport. The time had come to say goodbye and I looked at Max. Her black eyes fixed me like two overwhelming magnets. The intensity of their silent and motionless surge was such that I feared I would take her in my arms, or that she would burst into tears. I have never looked so deeply into a person's soul. Nor so beautifully.

I hastily shook hands, bid farewell and turned my back, so powerful are the habits of conventional manners and the tradition of restrained understatement. That look would haunt me for days. As we changed planes three hours later in Hong Kong, I did send Max a private email to thank her for the friendship and kindness during our stay in Guangzhou and Beijing. Four hours later, when I checked in at the hotel in Kaoshiung and could access the internet, I had a reply.

2. The Middle East, June

Nature gave me reasonably good looks. Some said I had the features of Harrison Ford. Or rather, considering our respective ages, Mr Ford had mine. Green eyes added to an appearance that caused occasional interest from ladies. The cool exterior, however, covered a tormented character and a stressed personality. The calmness of my gaze was a façade. Peace for me was in the solitude of mountains and the apparent emptiness of the sea. There wasn't much serenity elsewhere. My astrological sign is Gemini which some say accounts for dual and occasionally conflicting dispositions. I wanted to be a hero and I have succumbed to cowardice, I wanted to be noble, and I have been mean. I gave trouble where I meant help, and heartache where I intended love. I'm still somewhat surprised that a few people have developed a liking for me.

Max delicately expressed the pleasure she had in meeting us. Her attentions were natural, and she was hoping to see us again, regardless of business. She had appreciated our free talking in the suburbs and would welcome further advice.

Emails started flying back and forth, at first daily, and then more freely and frequently as the subjects warranted. Some messages were short, some elaborate, sharing experiences that I thought might be relevant to the career of a Chinese country girl. Max seemed grateful and appreciative of my communications. Her replies soothed my old unsettled soul. Soon my first business gesture in a workday would be to eagerly open the laptop and download the messages of the night. My home is in Bahrain, five hours behind Beijing. Therefore by the time I sat at my desk, my favorite export manageress had already sent a gently demanding note.

Max's company was due to exhibit its products at the Hannover Fair in June. I encouraged Max and her boss to stopover in the Middle East and explore our market on their way. We could also develop a partnership for marketing their products in Bahrain. We had good contacts in the country and a strategy was under development. The idea made sense and soon Max confirmed that we would see each other again. There was a sense of elation in our exchanges. I had promised her an outing in my sailboat if she stopped over in Manama.

I had of course wondered for some time about my position. I more than fancied this little black-eyed, short-nosed and straight-haired engineer. But was it sensible to admit it? What prospect would there be for a couple like us? On the one hand a Chinese creature of thirty years of age, on the other an old married misanthrope hailing from Western Europe and residing in the Middle East. Would that be fair on her?

My doubts and scruples couldn't resist a craving for intimate communication and for the sweetness of her responses. I eventually dared to venture that I had feelings towards her, that I appreciated her wisdom and human qualities. She acknowledged and responded in kind, always in a gentle and proper, genuine and spontaneous way. Thus encouraged I became bolder and one day of exuberance, I declared myself.

"I love you Max," I wrote to conclude one message.

"I love you, Long Nose," she replied.

Our exchanges became sweet and tender, in a curiously polite and restrained manner. The likelihood of seeing each other was improving as well as Max, her boss and a colleague were now committed to the Hannover Fair, and the stopover in Manama on their way back was becoming a certainty.

By then I was also planning to change jobs and I had the opportunity of a short break away from business, to spend as I wished. Over the years, I had developed a taste for trekking and looking at old stones. A good friend was managing a polo club near Jakarta, so I decided to spend a week in Indonesia, walking up a mountain or two, playing polo if I had a chance, visiting Borobudur, which I had wanted to do for a long time.

I asked Max in one of my emails if she would join me. Our chat in the suburbs of Beijing had established our common penchant for mountain walks. To my delight, she said yes, and we started making plans. Her stopover in Bahrain by mid-June would enable us to work out the details.

As the time of her arrival grew nearer, our excitement grew greater. Our feelings were in the open. The day finally arrived; it was now my turn to meet her at the airport. All my dreams and fantasizing were becoming reality!

*

As always, reality is an anti-climax. When she appeared at the gate, Max was a normal, somewhat ordinary and rather short person, carrying a shopping bag, walking normally between her two colleagues, and talking normally in her assured and down-to-earth manner. The presence of her boss and assistant killed any notion of romance. We exchanged polite greetings. I had developed a manly relation with Max's boss, and he, in turn, was calling me his brother. We slapped each other's shoulders and walked to the car park as old friends. In the car, Max sat in the back and I had to sit askew to see her in the rearview mirror.

They stayed at a hotel in Manama and we had the usual business routine of meetings, presentations, lunches, dinners and exchanges of gifts. The Chinese party named me Lee Zhu and gave me a beautifully carved seal, the surname being Max's touch, intended to pin me down in some lopsided manner. Mr and Mrs Lee?

During a car ride with Abdullah driving, I was alone with Max on the back seat and placed my hand on her thigh. She stiffened but I could sense the vibrations of her body. During meals, I occasionally played footsies and she responded eagerly each time, always keeping a very professional straight business face. We could freely hold hands in the car but not much more and we had to be content with that.

As the Friday came, I took Max for a sail in my dinghy. The boat, Titanic II, had been christened on account of its remarkably small size. Only 12 feet in length, it was very light and had the manners of a feather in any wind exceeding ten knots. The possibility sitting, albeit uncomfortably, was its sole advantage over a sailboard. Nevertheless, sailing the boat was an adventure for my little guest. She helpfully attended to the rigging and concentrated on my instructions. We set off in a light breeze and tacked a couple of times to let her get the feel of the environment. We cruised along the beach near the deep sea port, and after a while I could sense her relaxing a little. She remained very much on her guard, though, in the strange surroundings of a very small and low craft, in plain view of the swimmers on the beach, and in the company of a would-be lover playing at captain.

As the breeze dropped further, we laid down in the hull, waiting for the Titanic to round the breakwater and take us slowly back to the shore. My hand ventured on her leg again, and I eventually kissed her lips. Max wasn't unwilling but the setting must have been too strange. Her lips hardly parted and she remained somewhat rigid. Still, this was a first in our relationship, and a milestone in the logbook of the Titanic. She didn't comment but I conjectured that the open space, the low hull and the proximity of the beach were too much for her prude upbringing. Be that as it may, the trip became a cherished memory to be mentioned a few times in our correspondence.

We spoke about Indonesia. I asked about her way of life and, if on the one hand I was delighted to share a holiday with her—incidentally my first such "flint" ever, if flint is the appropriate word—on the other hand I was conscious of imposing a huge and costly constraint on Max's professional duties and personal budget. When I offered to buy her ticket and meet her costs, she was extremely firm in her rejection. To this day I hope I didn't offend her. Max had pride and dignity. We agreed however on timetables and meeting points.

With the coming and going associated with a hectic schedule, I had two occasions to see Max alone in her hotel room. Being together in a secluded place was a thrill, even if it was spoiled by the short time allowed in circumstances: twenty minutes on the first occasion, thirty on the second. We kissed clumsily and held each other. Max was very proper and well-mannered as always and I respected her too much—I still do—to push my male luck. I also knew that daring caresses could lead to frenzy and embarrassment. I forced myself to remain composed and our two opportunities for passion went up in puffs of outdated respectability.

"Sorry, Long Nose, we cannot be with you on Sunday, we have to meet a client." A small disappointment. Max's presence had become a feature of my life. With our talks of co-operation having gone very well, at least in terms of generalities, I had also taken it for granted that Max's activities in the region were focused on me and on the company I was running. Her company had its business which is none of mine. So, sure, Max, I will see you tonight and take you to the airport. Then I will see you in Jakarta and we will be able to love each other…

We parted company with a formal handshake, the despondency in our eyes somewhat mitigated by the promise of Indonesia two weeks later.

*

With her gone, life became flat again. The daily chores had no flavour, and the sun would shine only when she called or when I received an email.

Then two days before my flight to Jakarta, we received a fax from China: Max's company was confirming the principle of granting the agency of their products to the other party, met on the last day of their stay, subject to sales performance over the coming six months. The fax was addressed to their client and had been misdirected to us by a clumsy or ignorant fax operator in their Beijing office.

I had to read the cursed fax several times before I could figure out the story and its implications. Battle wounds hurt after a while. First there is a shock, an impact. My mind went blank for some time, then anger crept in, then anger grew into seething fury.

How could they do this thing? What the hell is the meaning of calling me Mr Lee, and being the "brother" of their president? To hell with the cunning devious duplicitous fork-tongued lying bastards!

I sent Max a curt and formal fax in return, demanding an explanation of the agreement with the competing company and asking why the fax was sent to us. I got an unsatisfactory and labored reply: the fax had come to us by mistake, and the promise to our competitor was conditional upon achieving sales targets. This did not conflict (my foot!) with the gentleman's (my foot again) agreement between them and us. The explanation did nothing to cool me down.

I told Max by email that I was extremely disappointed by the double-talk, and that I was feeling betrayed. I couldn't care less whether she would come to Indonesia, and that I would stop corresponding. I wiped my laptop clean of all previous correspondence with her.

She rang a couple of times. I could tell it was her from the display on the screen of my mobile. I did not pick up the phone.

3. Indonesia and Singapore, 1-5 July

I couldn't reconcile the cursed fax story with Max's personality. I had seen her in real life for about two weeks and we had exchanged dozens of messages. She was sweet, professional, dignified, honest, cheerful, intelligent, sensitive, compassionate, curiously fragile in some ways, yet strong in her mind, active, gentle and straightforward. And I still loved her.

1 July arrived. Already at Manama airport, I was wondering whether Max would be in Jakarta or not. According to the initial plan, her flight from Singapore was to land one hour ahead of mine. Therefore I would have caught up with her in the luggage reclaim area or at the arrival gate. Would she be there or not? My anger had closed the door for communication so I would not know about her reaction till I saw her, or not if she had taken exception at my brutal reaction.

On the one hand, I was still mystified and angry at the charade with our competitor, on the other, I was longing for the smile and easy friendship of my little Chinese would-be lover. The bottom line was that deep down, and no matter what the story of the fax was, I had already forgiven her and I was mad at myself for my display of temper. If she was there, I would hold her in my arms, and that was it. I mulled over that theme for most of the long flight to Jakarta.

*

Both Peter, my local polo friend, and the travel agency had assured me that an entry visa would be given on arrival. I walked confidently to the immigration desk that said "Visa on arrival", paid the 25 dollars fee and handed my passport to the immigration officer. He had a quick look and, standing up, he asked me to follow him to a secluded office. There an austere-looking official told me that the visa-on-arrival facility wasn't available to my nationality. He produced a list showing who had to apply to an Indonesian diplomatic representation office in their country of abode. He suggested that I should go back to Bahrain. Upon my incredulous and vehement reaction, he suggested that I could try the Indonesian embassy in Singapore.

Damn, damn, damn. What kind of fucked-up country is this? I had seen from the list that they would allow in Portuguese, Danes, Greeks and other nondescript nationalities, and not us? My protestations met with deaf ears, a well-tested technique for getting rid of nuisance travelers. They herded me back to the Gulf Air ground staff to ensure my departure on the return flight to Bahrain.

Infuriated and rattled, I tried to call Peter—thank God my mobile was working, but not his!—and then Max. And then the fourth miracle happened. She was at the arrival gate, waiting for me. Thank you, God. My ill-advised anger about the misdirected fax had not detracted her from meeting me. And she understood the visa problem, and yes she would find Peter and try to resolve this absurd situation.

I stalled the immigration guys as well as the Gulf Air ground staff, objecting to being bundled on the flight back and wanting to see what other options I had. Eventually, Max found Peter, also waiting at the arrivals gate, and we could talk over Max's phone. Peter was as mystified as I was about the visa problem. He called whoever he knew in the Indonesian establishment, but to no avail at this late hour (it already was 9pm). Eventually Peter talked his way through security, customs and immigration to come and greet me in the departure lounge. The options were limited: I already was a "cause célèbre" in the airport and there was no chance of reversing the decision of the officers, not even with a diplomatic twenty-dollar note inserted in my passport.

The choice was to go back to Bahrain and scrap the holiday, or go to Singapore to get a visa, and come back to spend whatever time was left of my break. The 1st of July was a Friday, so I would reach Singapore on the Saturday morning, stay put till the embassy opened on the Monday, and hopefully make it back the same day to Jakarta.

Well, what did I have to lose? I bought a ticket on a Singapore Airlines flight leaving for Changi at 7am. The immigration officers approved with gusto and led me to a bare room with a bench and a low table in a side corridor of the departure lounge. They didn't lock the door but there was a security guard not far away and I clearly topped his checklist.

*

I proceeded to waste the night away and was lying on the bench when a rattle of voices and quick steps shook me out of my slumber. The door was opened with vigor and a small group walked in the room, with Max in the middle. Before I had stood up and come to my senses, Max had thanked everybody and ushered them out. How she managed the feat of re-entering the airport and locating me in this hostile environment, I never understood clearly, even though she explained a few times. But then she's a strong, determined person.

To describe that night is impossible. The relief and elation of finding each other again after the drama of the fax, and the catastrophe of the visa were overwhelming. We held each other, we kissed, cuddled, looked at each other. She wanted to massage me to relieve the anguish; she wanted to sit at my feet; she wanted to hold me in my sleep.

Our demonstrations were subdued because of the security man and other staff passing by every once in a while. We had switched the light off and could snooze in the semi darkness. I caressed her and vividly remember my hand finding her smooth breast. Max was purring with the contentment of a cat curled in one's lap. The contrast between this sweet gentle cuddly kitten and the forceful lady who had bullied the airport staff was astonishing and poignant at the same time.

We slept badly but with our hearts content. Our intimacy didn't go far but we were in accord. Max told me more about the misdirected fax: her company was merely keeping its options open in case dealing with me wasn't successful enough. And, as I was changing company, Max felt she had no guarantee that my former company would do what I had committed? I was so rattled that I couldn't worry much longer about apparent Chinese duplicity and I kissed her again.

When the morning came, I promised to do my utmost to get a visa in Singapore by Monday. We left each other with a soul full of hope and a heart stamped with the memory of this improbable night.

*

I slept through most of the two days I had to kill in Singapore, though I did visit China Town and the Hindu temple in its midst.

I also called Max from time to time to distract our frustrated appetite for each other. I was staying at the Fujikama Hotel, where a Filipino band performed in the lobby every evening. As I was talking to Max, having a cool beer, she overheard the female singer in the background and got very agitated, suspecting I was in a karaoke bar.

Eventually she cooled down and accepted the explanation. Wow, the kitten had fangs!

The manager of the hotel travel agency promised to get a visa for Indonesia in a matter of hours, for S$100, which I happily committed. He was true to his word, and I made arrangements to take the 2pm flight from Singapore back to Jakarta on the Monday as I had hoped.

On Monday, I walked through the Indonesian immigration without hassle. Assholes!

*

Max was standing at the arrivals gate. We briefly embraced and started talking at the same time, shooting questions and answers in haphazard and hasty fashion, so much was our hunger for communication. We walked rapidly to the waiting car, to start the intended tour and at long last to be alone with each other.

The car was a tourism company van, driven by a cheerful and indefatigable character by the name of Dicky. His English was minimal but we didn't mind at all. We sat on the back seat and, blissfully indifferent to Dicky's travel plan, we held each other.

The plan was to get to a mountain resort for a night's stopover. We would proceed the next day to Yogyakarta, near Borobudur, and spend the Tuesday night in the Hyatt. On Wednesday, we would visit the temple, and in the afternoon get to the foot of the Merapi volcano which I wanted to climb. The Thursday evening would see us back in Jakarta by plane from Yogya. We would then spend the evening with Peter, and Max would return to China on the Friday morning. I would leave for Bahrain on the Friday night.

It was tight but manageable.

We left Jakarta airport at about 4pm. The drive to the mountain resort took till 3am the next day. That was one of the shortest journeys of my life. My happiness had created some magic environment where time, surroundings, hunger, discomfort and tiredness simply didn't exist. We talked, kissed, caressed, drank, ate, kissed, talked, slept, caressed, and drank, all in the relaxed, matter-of-fact manner of the inhabitants of heaven. Dicky ignored us and we didn't know he was there. The van rolled from side to side in the potholes of Indonesia countryside. Yet to us it was as if we were sitting on a cloud, frolicking with joy.

A sleepy watchman ushered us into the colonial-type resort. I had booked two rooms at all the hotels to preserve Max's modesty. Also, I didn't know whether she would want to share my bed and I had not asked her in those words. So the watchman handed me two keys. Max brushed the second key aside, and we found ourselves with ourselves, and nobody else, for the first time in this singular story.

*

Max came out of the bathroom wearing a silk robe. I kissed her feverishly, our passion about to culminate. Max smiled, remaining curiously shy; available and yet reserved; lightly dressed and mentally clad in armor. I could sense that sex was unfamiliar territory to her. I was very careful not to frighten her and to be gentle in every move. Her reserve was neither frigidity, nor fear, nor rejection. There was some kind of expectation that had to be satisfied to reach the next level. Love was like one of those fairy tales where a door leads to another door to another door to another door. Yet, with each door, the passion was growing.

Perhaps I have not done justice to Max's physical appearance. Her face was round and rather stern when she was intent on business. Her smile, however, was like the sun in the sky. As Chinese people go, at about 5-foot-4, she was taller than most and had a beautifully-shaped body with a smooth skin.

I have read Playboy, the Art of Love, Dangerous Liaisons, the Kama Sutra and the decadent Victorians. I have been married twice and had several girlfriends. I have seen blue movies and hard porn. I have been around and I'm not young. Never, ever have I had such a magnificent human experience as the one Max gave me. She offered herself, little by little, and yet totally in the end, in a gentle, positive way, with gratitude, with élan, with joy, with love, with care, with application, with interest, with modesty and yet with out-and-out participation. We made love more times that night than I had in the previous year. We fell asleep, inebriated with the heavenly drinks of passion.

*

We woke with the song of birds in the foliage. We made love again in an urgent manner, as if to reassure ourselves that we were together still. Then we got up, out and about. The hotel was nested in a magnificent landscape of jungle-covered hills, with a volcano towering above the horizon. Around, nature was lush, rich, and everywhere oozing life and freshness. We walked in the small park underneath the restaurant. We were like kids out of school. We were laughing for nothing. The world was ours.

As we walked along a low hedge, Max picked up long leaves and started weaving them into a small object as we progressed. After a while she handed it out to me. It was a ring. A cloud obscured the sky for a few seconds and the warm air appeared to cool down. Max said "Never mind" or something to that effect. I felt a touch of sadness and hypocrisy.

Actually I felt like a goddamned cheat towards two remarkable women.

*

Having toured the grounds of the hotel, we placed our fate once again in the hands of Dicky and resumed our flirting on the back seat of the van. The journey continued happily across the Indonesian countryside. We ate lunch in a small city, relaxed and contented like children on holiday.

In the evening we arrived at the Yogyakarta Hyatt. The hotel was magnificent: grand and picturesque, luxurious and comfortable. We settled in the room, showered and changed, feeling civilized again after our epic night journey. We checked emails and sent faxes, as professionals do as second nature. We had a drink or two in the bar of the hotel.

And then we talked about us, and Max started to cry. I suspected that she might not be able to hold her drink very well, nor her emotions. She started to cry, and continued, and continued. Reasoning had no effect. Reason has nothing to do with love, with instinct, or with passion.

During a pause in her distress, we entered the dining room. She spoiled her dish with enduring tears. No amount of comfort would detract Max from her distress. We skipped dessert and walked back to our room. By then Max had consumed her half of the wine I had ordered with the meal. That and the anguish at our situation was too much for her. She was about to start a fuss in the corridor, so I lifted her in my arms and carried her the last twenty meters to the room. We embraced on the bed, without removing our clothes. I drank her tears.

When we woke, somehow in peace, she didn't remember the night.

4. Yogyakarta and Merapi, 6–7 July

We drove in the bright sunshine of a beautiful day. I was curious about the Krator, the palace of the Sultan of Yogya, much vaunted in my tourist guide. Dicky dutifully dropped us at the gate where we paid the few rupiahs required to access the premises. The place wasn't quite worth the effort: low, vaguely exotic buildings sheltered the photo collection and paraphernalia of a backwater ruler, almost an ex-one for that matter. A mention of his harem of eighty wives left Max unimpressed, since she disapproved of harems in the first place, and in the second, being fiercely Chinese, she probably thought that the Chinese emperors, with their thousands of concubines, were clearly superior to these village tyrants.

We left the Krator without regret and proceeded to Borobudur, about one hour's drive away. The car park was already full of vendors of souvenirs, curios, postcards, and shirts. Their sales pitch was overwhelming and it took a very determined stance to keep them at bay. The entrance fee for foreigners, being in dollars, was quite steep whilst natives benefited from a subsidized tariff. However, I didn't mind the charge as much as the crowd that roamed around the monument.

The temple itself was massive but it impressed most from a distance. At close quarters, it was an endless bas-relief of stone carvings with significance for the scholar only. I didn't experience the awe inspired by the pyramids, nor the harmony at the Parthenon. Max dutifully followed my steps, as always kindly agreeing to whatever plan I had or change of plan I wanted. On the way out she bought me a booklet about the monument in English and Chinese.

Finishing with tourist duties, we set out for the Merapi volcano. I picked the mountain because of its position relative to Yogya (35km north), its height (3,000m), and its general description in my tourist handbook. Merapi is an active volcano. According to the handbook, the climb takes four hours from the village of Selo, on the north slope, where a lodge offers shelter to trekkers, and where guides are available. I had naively surmised that the travel agency mobilized by Peter would have made a booking at the lodge and that a guide would be waiting for us.

That assumption was naïve indeed. We reached Selo after a winding drive on the lower reaches of the mountain. The deserted, soulless hamlet had no visible lodge and no tourist office. Dicky didn't understand any of our expectations. The travel agency evaded the calls from our mobile phones. As we were idling at the beginning of the trek leading to the summit, a couple of would-be guides offered their services, explaining the routine of the climb. Departure would be at 1am to reach the summit in time for sunrise. We would have to equip ourselves with torches, water, snacks and waterproof clothing. Well, well, well. And where is the Selo lodge? Dicky shook his head. No lodge. I provisionally booked a guide for 1am and we held a war council.

Resourceful as always, I grabbed the handbook and re-read the page on Merapi. There was another point of access to the mountain at the south slope, from a village called Kaliurang, which also had a lodge and a hotel. We decided to try it. On the drive out of Selo we noticed too late a nondescript house with a huge totem-like sign that said "Hotel". But by then we were committed in our minds to a climb from Kaliurang on the dubious grounds that it couldn't be worse than the trek from Selo.

During yet another long, winding drive around the mountain it began to rain and there was a chill in the air. However, the back seat of the van was still comfortable and we knew how to keep each other warm. The drive took over an hour yet still it didn't last long. For lovers, time has less tediousness than for other humans.

When we reached it at about 6.30pm Kaliurang was dark and uninviting. There was a hotel all right, but it had no running water, no reservations from our travel agency and no guide. A light rain continued to fall. Eventually an old man appeared and advised us that the south side of the volcano wasn't accessible because of flowing lava. There was a possible walk of about one hour to reach an altitude of 1,400 meters from where tourists could view the summit in the distance. No thank you! We bought torches, snacks and water in a nearby shop and, having resumed our position on the back seat of the van, instructed Dicky to take us back to Selo, with a mind to try the hotel with the totem-like advertisement and to depend on the provisional arrangement with the guide whose name we didn't even know.

Another winding drive. We had to admire Dicky's patience and composure as he took us back and forth around the volcano. The rain didn't stop. By the time we finally reached Selo again and its minuscule hotel, it was 9 pm, the rain was pounding hard, and the air was cold. A single large room was at the same time the reception, the lounge and the restaurant. An old lady checked us into a schoolbook register. The hotel had a thatched roof which leaked water, so that we had to move the paper coffee cups right and left to catch the more persistent leaks. The bamboo tables and benches suggested a large population of cockroaches.

I do not know what Max may have been thinking at that particular time. She seemed to have an unshakeable faith in my judgment and decision-making, for she appeared unruffled. However, I was fairly perplexed at our situation. True to my usual reckless attitude I had no waterproof clothing, let alone warm protection, the deal with our guide wasn't really a firm arrangement and the climb was definitely more daunting than the handbook had suggested.

A middle-aged villager walked into the hotel and started chatting up the old lady. After a while he turned round and introduced himself in good English: "I'm Superman. How are you?" and he handed us a card saying SUPERMO "Superman" Authorized Mountain Guide. He offered his services, fetched ponchos for us made of polythene sheets and in no time at all my gloomy outlook took a turn for the better. Only the rain was continuing to dampen my spirits. Superman advised us that we should rest in our room and he would fetch us at 1am to get started if the rain had stopped.

We went to bed at about 11pm in a crude room with a large bed. We lay down in our clothes and went uneasily to sleep. After a while, Superman woke us to say that with the rain unabated, he would check us again at 2am. If it was still raining, we would abort, if the rain had stopped, we would get going.

At 2am, the rain had stopped. Not one hundred percent, but enough for Superman to pretend that it wasn't falling anymore. We set off, tired and sleepy, with cold in our bones. Dicky, forever on duty, drove us from the hotel to the starting point of the trek, some three kilometers away, at an altitude of 1,900 meters. And we started the walk.

For some romantic reason, I was wearing the old boots I had used on the Kilimanjaro climb a couple of years earlier. Fairly worn out, their soles had no grip in the muddy soil and I was slipping painfully at every step. In the weak light of the torch, we could see rivulets running down the steep muddy slope. Rainwater was dripping from the foliage overhead and wet leaves brushed against us from the sides of the path. By the time I put on the poncho, my shirt and trousers were thoroughly soaked. With inadequate physical training my breathing was labored from the start and my heartbeat soon ran out of control. I had the embarrassment of calling for repeated rests to catch my breath. Max and Superman kindly obliged. Then the rain started again. My torch was failing, and with water droplets on my glasses, my vision was blurred, which made my slipping worse, which in turn increased my breathlessness. I felt miserable and helpless.

Then, little by little, my muscles warmed up and removing my glasses allowed me to see better. After two hours of misery, the agony lessened a bit and I got into a steadier pace. Superman, in front and obviously high on kryptonite, was walking at a quarter of his natural speed and looked exceedingly bored.

Between 4 and 5am the rain stopped for good. After a while we could see a pale light in the east and the darkness surrounding us started to reveal the shapes of trees and rock outcrops. Faint lights became visible in the valleys below. The ground turned from muddy clay to lava. The vegetation thinned out and Superman declared that we were approaching the plateau, from where the view of the sunrise was best. The daylight was now stronger. Clouds drifted below and above. At last, the Merapi's cone became visible, black and forbidding. A white plume of smoke or water vapor was hanging over the lip of the crater.

The plateau, at an altitude of 2,600 meters, offered a balcony from where to look at a stunning landscape. The towering scree slope topped by the smoke, the layers of cloud to the left, the deep valleys around, all made for a breathtaking panorama.

Then a bright red blade cut through the layers of cloud to the east. The light became stronger. The red blade became a giant blinding sword of light, red and yellow. The entire world took life as if reborn. A stunning rainbow materialized to the west. The scene was magnificent beyond words. The tiredness of the night disappeared in the communion with primeval nature. We took pictures. I changed into the dry clothes that I had carried in my rucksack. We ate snacks and drank water. We took more pictures. We had joy in our hearts.

Superman pointed towards the continuing track up the scree slope. There was another 400 meters of vertical climb to reach the summit of the crater. He also gave me a peculiar look. Obviously I had not made a strong impression as a climber. He talked about the time it would take to complete the climb. We wisely decided to walk down.

Having left the plateau between 6.30 and 7am, we reached the bottom at 9.30. The last mile was excruciatingly painful as my knee joints gave way. I was limping at a very slow pace, and Superman was now clearly exasperated. Max wanted to help and we had a short argument as to who should carry the rucksack. Peasants were walking up the volcano slopes to tend their fields.

Brave Dicky was duly waiting for us where the trek rejoined the road. God bless him. I often reflected how life could give acute pain one moment, and then one step later, the legs are blissfully stretched on the back seat of a van and the pain already only a memory.

Back at the hotel, we washed as best we could with a pail of water. The old lady had prepared omelettes with chilies, bread and coffee. It was a delicious meal. Food in the stomach and ointment on the knees made me a new man, despite the lack of sleep. We sat again on our favorite back seat and Dicky took us on the last leg of our motoring tour of Indonesia.

We ate lunch in a country restaurant. A gentle, smiling waitress set up mats on the floor in the center of a small open pavilion built in the middle of a quiet pool. We were tired from the night of walking, with stiff legs and aching backs. Yet our souls were content. The world was ours. Actually we didn't need the world. The food was spicy and the beer cool. The hour was perfect.

5. Jakarta, 8-9 July and the Middle East Later

His mission over, Dicky dropped us at Yogya airport. We tipped him well. He will live long in our memory. We caught a flight back to Jakarta. Peter's driver met us and by 7.30pm we were in the Ibis Hotel. A shower removed the grime from Merapi. It felt strange that, hardly twelve hours earlier, we were straggling down the muddy slopes of a volcano. The mud disappeared in the shower drain and clean clothes made us feel completely refreshed.

Peter was at the bar of the hotel, waiting for us. Our adventures provided small talk for an hour or so. Then Peter took us on a tour of the city. We saw the lines of ancient schooners that had plied the southern sea lanes, the original Batavia bridge, and eventually had a wonderful dinner in the old Jakarta Club with its magnificent bar and wood-paneled dining room. During the meal, Peter challenged Max about Tiananmen. She didn't give an inch. They didn't take to one another after that exchange.

By dessert we were truly done. We had slept only two hours the previous night and had walked for a solid seven hours under strenuous conditions. We wanted a bed. Back at the Ibis, we made love with the awareness of our separation the next day. There was a sense of urgency in our holding onto each other. Even though we were very tired, Max set her alarm clock for 6am so that we would lose as little as possible of each other's presence.

The shrill sound of the alarm drilled through my tired brain. Immediately I felt Max's arms around me and her body pressing against mine for more intimacy. We made love again like drowning swimmers embracing a buoy.

Then work instincts prevailed. There was a flight to catch, people to meet. We got out of bed and readied ourselves. Max was catching a flight to Singapore and I was meeting Peter at the polo club.

Peter's driver was on time, that is not too late. He took us to Jakarta airport. Max kissed me briefly and walked into the terminal without looking back. I knew she would have cried if she had. Me too, probably.

I spent the rest of the day with Peter at the polo field. The setting was magnificent and screamed for a glamorous (and profitable) real estate development. And then maybe it didn't. Beautiful nature and exhilarating sport can do without snobbery. We had a relaxed lunch at the adjacent golf club. We talked some more and then the time came for me as well to leave. With a heavy heart I bid farewell to my friend and to the country of which I had seen so little and which loomed so large in my mind.

At the departure lounge I could access the internet and sent Max a message. I said with all my heart that despite the commercial treason of her firm, despite the visa mix-up, despite the discomfort of the night in the Jakarta airport, despite the wait in Singapore, despite the bumpy endless drives on the roads of Indonesia, despite the pain of the climb on Mount Merapi, despite the tears in the wine at Yogyakarta, I never ever had such a wonderful holiday. With all my heart. And I loved her.

*

She replied that she had cried on the flight back, but she was strong and she loved me too.

Our exchanges became free from the inhibitions of platonic lovers. So we talked more freely about sex, about passion, about us. I teased her about my performance, suggesting that I had made love to her so many times during her night of inebriation. She appeared to believe my bragging.

Our feelings grew in depth and in substance. Their expression became more frequent as well. We would exchange twenty messages in a day. Her contact became a drug. Every day my first action would be to open the laptop and check for her messages. She sent the photographs taken in Indonesia, one or two a day, which made us live through the epic vacation over and over again. The view of the sunrise on Merapi was stunning.

The correspondence was in turn romantic, light-hearted, passionate and teasing, but it was always plentiful. Questions would be answered in minutes. Then answers would be demanded in seconds. Kisses would fly the internet in bundles on any occasion and in any circumstance.

It had been obvious from many aspects of our relations that Max had had a very conservative upbringing, where nakedness, sex and related topics were taboo. That was a source of tenderness for me, of interest as well as I enjoyed letting her discover the world. She had told me over and over again that she was impressed by my experience of life and the wisdom of my judgments. If only she knew my self-doubts! Anyway, the exchanges were intense, pleasant and frequent.

But the exchanges were not really leading anywhere.

*

My new job in Qatar entailed the re-organization and development of a medium-size construction company. We had new projects in hand to be started, and new prospects for which we had to mobilize partners of suitable strength and capability. The chairman suggested Chinese partners.

I seized the opportunity. I asked Max to research the Chinese market for the equipment needed on our new building sites and I asked her boss, my brother, to identify potential partners for large developments due to start in Qatar. Both set out to work on our requirements and the flow of business messages soon nearly equaled the volume of romantic notes. I was to combine a journey to Beijing with a trip to Bombay to recruit staff for the new projects.

On the evening of 1 September, I was on my way to India where my good friend Mr Vikram had arranged several interviews. I would arrive in Mumbai early on the Friday, conduct the screening of recruits on Friday and Saturday morning, flying to Beijing on the Saturday night with the hope of spending much of the Sunday with Max.

Vikram, a perfect host, took me to an excellent Chinese restaurant in Mumbai—a good omen, I thought. My business in India was concluded as planned and I went to Mumbai airport. At the lounge I sent a burning message to Max, telling her of my passion and that I wanted our lovemaking to culminate in total fusion of our two beings. I wanted my seed to penetrate every molecule of hers, and my sex to reach her soul. I asked her when we would be by ourselves, to stand still, not uttering a word. I saw her with her eyes closed, trusting me. I boarded the flight to Hong Kong with my mind focused on the coming encounter.

The Air India flight was as bad as could be. The only items on board in common with normal airlines were the toothpicks and the airsickness bag.

6. Beijing and the Chinese Countryside, 4–8 September

True to form, Air India ran late in reaching Hong Kong and I missed the connection to Beijing. I mentally downgraded the merits of their toothpicks and airsickness bags. However, there was another flight one hour later that I could catch and I managed to tell Max over the phone about this setback. She was professional as always; handling visitors was second nature to her. So I waited for the new departure time.

At long last I was through the arrivals gate at Beijing airport. I immediately noticed David, Max's tall assistant, and then Max next to him. Instead of straight black hair and conventional clothes, Max now had curls and was wearing a black stylish Chinese dress. She was looking gorgeous.

We greeted each other as old friends and proceeded to the Tianlun Dynasty Hotel where I had stayed in April. The president of Max's company, my brother, had made a point of coming to greet me at the hotel, so we all had to go through a light meal when none of us, I believe, was hungry. Certainly I wasn't, having had so many meals and snacks in planes and airport lounges. Eventually the rigmarole was over and my hosts departed, Max indicating in a short aside that she would be back as soon as she could. I had made a point that the overnight journey had been long and tiresome and I was aspiring to a quiet rest. Fifteen minutes after I had settled in the room, Max turned up.

Our passion had been initiated by the wonderful but very short holiday in Indonesia; it had been fueled by our daily correspondence, and it was about to be satisfied, if love can ever be.

*

I closed the door behind her with one hand and held Max with the other. We kissed in the fashion of drowning people gasping for air. The room was made of a short narrow passage with the hanging cabinet to the left and the bathroom to the right. We stood there embracing for a long time. She had closed her eyes while I kissed her face, her neck and her lips again. I fumbled with the zippers and other fasteners of her dress and bra. Eventually I had access to the smoothness of her breasts and belly. She was still immobile, swaying slightly under my caresses. Still we had not moved, not even by one step from the moment we held each other. The joy of discovering and re-discovering was overwhelming.

In the end I couldn't resist any longer and I lifted her in my arms, as I had done in the corridor of the Yogyakarta Hyatt, to bring her to the bed. She still had her eyes shut. I removed her remaining clothes as well as mine and the miracle happened again. Never ever have I had sex so complete, so full, so long, so intense, so rewarding, so sweet, so unforgettable and so shared. We rested between embraces, drinking each other's sweat, only to start again in a never-ending dream. We got out of a ravaged bed in the evening for dinner. Tiredness and a happy daze were to be the features of this trip for me. I would be exhausted and yet on a permanent high for the next four days. I do not recall the food eaten that evening, but I recall we went back to bed and carried on through the night.

*

The next day saw us in Max's offices, meeting with salesmen and with a representative of the potential joint venture partner. We had a busy time and my brother, Mr Shang, had set his mind to round it off in the evening with a treat: he was adamant that I should have a sauna-massage-health treatment with him at his favorite establishment.

Max was very agitated at the prospect, being very suspicious of the proceedings behind the closed doors of the parlor. There was no escape, however, and I had to commit to the evening.

We had a slow start. The meeting with Mr Shang at the health center was fixed for 10pm or so. After the business meetings, Max and David took me out for a stroll in the vicinity of the Dynasty Hotel. We had a snack in a Japanese fast food joint which was to upset me for several days with a severely runny tummy. I had a faint suspicion that Max may have conspired to create my condition to incapacitate me in case of a "special" massage. Be that as it may, after some window shopping and banter near the hotel, the time of the treat arrived and Mr Shang picked me up together with David as translator. Max saw us off with a stern look on her face. No matter what re-assurance I had given, she had little faith in men and in girls of massage parlors.

As it was, the proceedings involved little that could have concerned Max. Attendants gave us slippers, and then took us to a locker room where we undressed completely. We entered a huge lounge with a pool and baths in the center surrounded by showers and cubicles similar to those of a hair dressing salon. I could see a sauna at the far end. Some fifty or maybe a hundred naked men were milling around. The sight was truly astonishing to me. I did my best to retain my composure, not too sure whether I was more embarrassed at my public nakedness, or amused at so much flabby flesh and so many hanging organs. I had a shower, followed by a sauna, after which I dressed in tight flesh-colored underwear and a bathrobe, and played a lengthy game of table tennis in the large play-cum-restaurant area. The premises were surprisingly large and elaborate.

Then it was time for the massage proper. Each massage cabinet was like a regular hotel room and I was told that some customers would simply stay in the establishment, not bothering with a normal hotel. The person in attendance was a smiling girl, speaking basic English. I removed the bathrobe but kept the tight-fitting underwear, feeling vaguely idiotic in the attire. I'm not a fan of massage parlors, but I have visited some. Till now I have not found the balance between embarrassed self-consciousness if I'm naked, and excessive caginess if I'm not.

The girl, however, wasn't perturbed by my unease. She gave me a thorough work-out and after a while—I think I slept for some time—she indicated that the session was over. Mr Shang had emerged from his own session and took me in tow again, in the direction of the restaurant. By then I had already developed serious indigestion, courtesy of the Japanese fast food. I did my best to oblige, washed down whatever food I was offered with cold beer, and gratefully went to bed at 2.30am. We were due to fly to Wei Hai, a city about 500 miles east of Beijing, to visit the factory that would manufacture our equipment. Take-off was at 7.30 or 8am.

*

The flight was uneventful, and the discovery of the Chinese countryside was a thrilling prospect, were it not for the absurdly short night, and the continuing stomach upset.

The city of Wei Hai is nested on the Pacific Ocean between green, rolling hills. The place is attractive and well developed. The local airport looked very much like the one in Geneva. The factory staff welcomed us and we had a grand tour of the facilities. We dispatched the business subjects with reasonable ease. The company chairman, appropriately named Mr Mao, invited us for a copious lunch during which countless toasts were given to each and sundry, including their company, country, family, and any other suitable drinking topic. By then my stomach was in real turmoil, and I restricted myself to strong drinks only, on the phony pretense that it would help settle my unruly belly. Avoiding food, though, was quite a challenge in the face of Chinese country hospitality.

The test drew to an end. In the evening, after the customary demonstrations of friendship with Chairman Mao, we took the return flight to Beijing.

By midnight we were back in bed, Max having ostentatiously wished me a good night in front of her president, only to return to the Dynasty Hotel through the back door. We made love again with urgency and obsession. We had to get up at 5.30am to drive to Anwan—a 6- or 7-hour drive out of Beijing—to have a look at a second-hand crane that we might want to buy.

*

The drive actually took more than nine hours. It was torture. By now my indigestion had turned to dysentery, painful, uncomfortable and dirty. Service stations and toilets, few and far apart, are designed for the intensive use of truck drivers. I suffered in silence, praying for stopovers with reasonable facilities. At one stage I asked for a stop at a clothing store to replace soiled garments. As this request turned out to be not quite practical in the Far East countryside, I had to live with my misery. A lunch break was no relief, except for the access to a better bathroom. We plodded on.

We finally reached the work site where we were to inspect the second hand rig by five pm. I made a weak pretense of interest and took a few photographs for the record. We got back to Beijing at 3.30am. I was drained of all fluids and thoroughly exhausted. I had a long shower to remove the filth and collapsed in Max's arms as she came back to the hotel, having yet again made an excuse to go home for the benefit of the driver. Mr Shang had arranged — and insisted — that I should be ready the next morning at 9am for a final meeting at the headquarters of the putative joint venture partner.

*

By 8am on the last day of my visit to China, I tore myself out of the embrace of my little Chinese cat. I had to shake the tiredness and the sore tummy out of my system to get ready and meet Andy, the mentor assigned by Mr Shang to the chore of the morning.

As it happened we came to the meeting with the prospective partner nearly an hour early and had to wait. I cursed the overzealous nitwit who had robbed me of much needed sleep and of an extra hour of Max's presence. Still I managed to conclude some useful business and was treated to a remarkably good lunch in their VIP dining room. Then came the time to make for the airport. Andy drove past Mr Shang's office where I had the opportunity of a despondent handshake with Max who was attending to her export manageress's duties.

The trip back from Beijing was long, punctuated by visits to airport-lounge toilets and stopovers at internet stations. By the next day I was back in Doha.

7. Doha, Autumn

By education I am a civil engineer specializing in construction. However, my career has been entirely dedicated to management activities. Over the past 12 years or so, following some success in the field of re-structuring, I found myself increasingly recognized as a company doctor. The recent assignment in Doha was one of those: the owners of the company had neglected their investment, the problems had mounted, there was no organization, staff morale was low and the financial situation appalling. I was hired to cure the ills of the company.

Sorting out the situation was a matter of hard work and time. Several complications had to be resolved, such as keeping in check the old-fashioned shareholders, averse to delegation and relishing in trifling details. Another difficulty was the country's boom: any professional worth his salt could easily find a new job, much better paid. Company executives would go back and forth between careers at a dizzying pace. With harrowing problems and elusive staff, my task at times felt fairly hopeless.

*

After the apotheosis of our last encounter, the mails to Max flew back and forth at an increased pace, there being bundles of kisses, suggestions of caresses and sexual innuendos to spice up the exchanges. Soon the correspondence became an absorbing activity, with growing demands for attention.

In parallel with the exigency of romance I found mounting and frustrating work pressure. Results failed to materialize, new solutions created new problems, and the initial honeymoon associated with a new management outlook turned sour as expectations were not immediately met. My natural patience grew shorter.

*

All along I wondered what future there was for Max and me. I was weary of her excessive attachment for her own good. The laws of nature are such that her life expectancy would exceed mine by several decades. Culturally, we were worlds apart and several misunderstandings had popped up as a result of her limited knowledge of English. Her life had to be centered away from Long Nose.

Was I another dirty old man, taking advantage of a younger girl? Am I still searching for an emotional balance? Was Max the person for me? Sure enough she was gentle, tolerant, intelligent and perceptive. Yet I harmed her unwittingly on occasions.

What is love? Is it infatuation? Sexual attraction? Empathy of the souls? Unity of material interests? A mix of them all? How did I get into that extraordinary story, and where would it lead her and lead me? Max had wanted a girl from me. Was that sensible in any way? For the child, for Max, for me?

I handle human relationships poorly. Perhaps the death of my father at a time when I needed him most had terminally impaired my ability to relate with other humans; perhaps also my ability to trust them, to depend on them. I don't know: I should become another human to judge that. However, seeing others' attitudes and performance, I had to conclude that I must be still a fairly ordinary guy. Like all others I'm subject to lust and the desire for honesty, to indolence and the desire to show off, to greed and attempts at generosity, to conceit and a sense of realistic modesty, to folly and the need for wisdom.

At times I find it difficult to live with myself.

*

With the workload accumulating through the passing weeks into unrelenting stress, I was losing the patience and the time to cope with the distractions of a love story. Something had to give. I needed space to reflect on the prospects of our relationship and the nature of my emotions.

About eight weeks after my return from Beijing, I called Max to tell her that I needed solitude. I asked for a respite in our communications, telephone calls and emails. I felt that I was hurting her badly. Somehow, the stress to which I was exposed had been showing and Max expected a consequence to my obvious difficulties.

Yet I felt like a heartless brute. She asked if I still loved her, and then, accepting my desperate need for introspection, she gently asked whether we could remain friends, regardless of the outcome of my seclusion.

*

For days and then weeks, I had Max on my mind, going over the same topics.

The period was intense, with hard business meetings, severe confrontations, challenges, and difficult decisions. Yet slowly, grindingly, life and work began to take shape. As for Max, the obvious and conflicting parameters remained unchanged. I wanted to be her friend forever, her lover for as long she wanted me. I didn't want to be the focal point of her life which had to revolve around China and her own environment. I'm too remote, physically and culturally, to fulfill the needs of her existence. Max, even though she does not know it or does not recognize it, is very strong. My only worthwhile contribution to her existence on this planet is to be the catalyst in releasing her power.

After three weeks of silence, I picked up the phone and punched the keys to call my little Chinese cat. She was waiting for my call. I do not know where this will lead us.

I pray I will not harm anyone.

BETRAYALS

The air conditioning had broken down again. Under the weak emergency light a sheen of perspiration glistened on Pol Pot's naked torso as he stood up from his bunk and, with an unsure gait, walked to the window. Through the iron grill, he stared at the lights of the city, seemingly at peace with itself. What peace?

The sticky heat had pulled him from an agitated sleep; the heat and the nightmare of course. It was always the same—peaceful fields tended by happy farmers, collective irrigation managed by benevolent cadres, plentiful crops, fat cattle, and in the distance the protection of the flag of Kampuchea, gently floating in the evening breeze. As always the vision disappeared under a thundering, howling hurricane. A heavy lid of black clouds shrouded the land. The roar of the storm filled the sky. In his dream, Pol Pot would cover his ears with his hands. When his heart and his head were about to explode, he would wake up, sweating and shivering.

*

Those judges and do-gooders, those victors who now write history, state that my political program was muddled. Of course they would say so. They have never been us, never been part of our creed. They are not our people. They have not seen the arrogant French trudging the realm of the Khmer kings. They have not lived the dreams of Chairman Mao and Uncle Ho. They have not marched the long march. They have forgotten Ghandi and his vision of a peaceful, gentle society where each man would weave his own cloak and grow his own food, far away from the corruption of cities, from the temptations of wealth and the fallacies of power.

The French left the country in the hands of King Norodom and his strong man, Marshall Lon Nol. Educated in Paris, Lon Nol had acquired the vices of his French masters without any of their rare virtues. Our fighters struggled for years in the jungle against the hideous inheritance of the colonial regime, countless times given for lost at the hands of Lon Nol's army of thugs. Always done in, always worn out, on the run, out of supplies. It took enormous faith, unflinching belief and superhuman courage to carry on through those endless, merciless years.

The soldiers were brutal: a comrade taken was a comrade beaten, tortured, and killed. Yet our fighters were heroes. Not only did they fight back, they also spread the word of the revolution and the gospel of the future. For each of our fighters tortured and killed, we tortured and killed three minions of Lon Nol. The countryside was washed in blood well before the outside world paid attention.

With the help of our Chinese brothers, little by little, we eroded the regime. Its army lost ground, its administration disintegrated, came apart at the seams. One glorious day, after twenty years in the wilderness, in an orgasmic culmination, we conquered Phnom Penh. Kampuchea was free. No, Kampuchea was born.

Over six passionate months, we worked to create a new world. We had to reward, to punish, to clean, to organize, to create. Heaven was possible. The cities had been the source of all evils: unemployment, poverty, prostitution, and sleaze. We decided to lose the cities. The future was waiting and we pressed on with the re-location of populations, re-building the rural society of our dreams.

And then everything went to pieces. The people had relished being destitute. They resented leaving their filth. We had to coerce them. The future would not wait forever. We had to purge the nation from its negative elements for the good of the masses. The people betrayed us and betrayed themselves.

Our cadres had to be brave again. They had to be ruthless in pursuing the revisionists and those attached to false values, herding the populace towards its new model. From the duties of rigorous shepherds, they embarked upon the chores of hellish hounds. They betrayed me and they betrayed themselves.

*

He grabbed the iron bars of the window, his gaze fixed on a future that would never be. Tears rolled down his cheeks.

JOHN WAS HERE

He closed his eyes. His mind drifted again.

Against the screen of his eyelids, he could still see the bare walls of dark blue limestone. On one side of the heavy oak door was the wooden frame of the bed with a single thin blanket. The prie-dieu, also of solid wood, was on the other side. A small table under a large crucifix and a chair completed the furniture of the cell. Opposite the door above an ancient radiator were two high narrow windows with stained glass. No curtains. A desk light with a green cover cast shadows across the flagstones of the floor. The arches of the ceiling stretched the walls into endless darkness.

The rumble of a cell door being closed echoed in the corridor of the cloister and suppressed for a moment the barely audible monks chanting the prayers of the evening office in the chapel. He could smell a trace of incense in the cold air.

He had renounced everything, cut all links. Peace was with him now. He had nothing, he needed nothing and nothing could hurt him. He had serenity. The Gregorian chant died and he heard the hushed steps of the monks walking back to their cells.

*

He kept his eyes closed. Once, years ago, he had tasted the tranquility of life in a monastery. He had been tempted.

Aom came back with a glass of whisky and placed it in his hand. He stirred on the couch, unsure that he wanted the reality of the world again. Resigned, he opened one eye. The room of course had not changed; the crumpled bed sheets that Aom had not bothered to tidy, the ceiling fan shifting warm humid air, the dark green of the immutable jungle canopy in the window, and the idle laptop a lifeless reproach on the bamboo table.

He pressed the cold glass against his perspiring forehead before taking a sip. The girl nudged herself against him. He placed his free hand on her breast and closed his eyes again.

THE PILGRIMAGE

1

Lhassa airport appeared under the wing of the plane. The runway stretched along the south bank of the Brahmaputra river, nestling between high ridges. The plane veered over the mountains and aligned its descent on the axis of the valley. The air was clean and the eye could capture summit after summit stretching to infinity, many still capped with snow.

As the tourist walked from the plane to the terminal building, he felt his head swimming in the rarefied oxygen of the altitude. His pace was lighter, slightly bouncy, and a bit uneven. The weighty grip of his life and duties had been shaken loose a little. The stresses of modern life seemed out of place and irrelevant in the quiet, unhurried environment of the empty airport. The guide from the travel agency greeted him and placed a long, white silk wrap on his shoulders in a gesture of embrace. He welcomed the acceptance and felt the weight of his past slipping further.

He reached the hotel after a leisurely ride. He had peered at the scenery, hypnotized by the novelty of it all: the endless sky, the brown mountains, the broad valley with shallow streams of water between flats of pebbles. Every once in a while, the taxi would overtake an agricultural tractor pulling a makeshift trailer, an overloaded tri-wheeler, or the odd cart pulled by a scrawny horse.

The sun had been warm on his face at the airport, but the hotel was in the shadow of the mountains and here the air was chill. He walked briskly to his room, hoping for some kind of heating. But there was none and he spent a dull evening wrapped in a blanket, eating cold spaghetti with hot tea, courtesy of a room service clearly overwhelmed by his demands. He went to bed early and spent the night shivering.

When he woke from a listless sleep, he had a headache. He decided that it should not spoil his day. The sun was streaming through the window and joy lifted his mind at the thought of a new day in a new world. He put shades on, swallowed a couple of aspirin and walked down to the breakfast room.

2

The old monk pulled the maroon robe tighter around his shoulders for better protection against the wind chill. The sun was bright on the mountain top, but at that height the airstream never relented. The novices had finished stretching wires from the masts and hanging prayer flags. The gay colors fluttered in the sky in their hundreds. He prepared to walk down, adjusting his spectacles at the top of his nose. He had a last look at the form they had disposed on a flat boulder, ready for its sky burial and journey to eternity. The wind had caught a corner of the shroud, exposing the face of the old peasant.

As the monk climbed back to the body, a large crow landed next to the exposed head and pecked at the eyelids. The monk picked up a stone and threw it to scare the bird. The black scavenger stepped back and flapped its wings. The monk shooed it away with large arms movements. He pulled the shroud back to cover the cadaver and ballasted it with a stone in a futile gesture. The monk walked down, not looking back. Soon he caught up with the novices and the family who had been waiting for him.

The walk back to the village would take three hours, plenty of time to think. He had to reprimand the novices, as usual carefree and playful, and heedless of the sorrow of the family. He resolved to talk to the abbot again. The young recruits of the monastery needed discipline, and discipline came from the top. Also, the funeral rites needed to catch up with the times and lose the legacy of ancient shamans. The Lord Buddha had not prescribed burial of humans by corpse-eating birds. The old monk had traveled the world and visited many monasteries, ashrams and convents. He had read many books and scriptures, talked to learned men and wise gurus. He had found the Indian practice of burning bodies the most respectful and dignified. India had been the cradle of the religion from where enlightenment had cast its light on the entire continent.

Yes, he would go to the abbot again. Too many things were not right. Religion was built on respect of individuals and respect of oneself. That was how it ought to be.

3

The tourist walked the two miles from the hotel to the Potala Palace. He was puffing heavily and his head had not cleared, but his eyes were filled with awe and wonder. The white walls reached to the sky. The stairs, portals, windows and balconies visible at the top conjured a vision of power and extra-terrestrial mystery. The thrill of entering a new world left a prickle along his spine.

There was a large crowd milling around the palace. Then he realized that the people were not actually milling, they were walking clockwise around the hill upon which the palace was perched—some fast, some at a leisure pace, some very slow. Some were chanting, in low-keyed voices; prayers, no doubt. He wove his way through the throng, reached the entrance and paid the modest fee. Slowly, he walked the many stairways to the top.

The first courtyard was majestic. Huge black screens made of dyed yak wool lined the walls. The was a large closed portico, painted in bright colors and inviting dreams. The view over the parapet was breathtaking. In the thin air, the landscape was crisp for miles and miles. The tourist could locate his hotel and, beyond, the plain with the Brahmaputra. He remembered the worn-out advert about Tibet being the roof of the world. From this terrace, he thought, any other place on earth was down there, somewhere way below. He was on top of the world. His headache was almost gone.

The tour continued with the visit of the chapels dedicated to each of the fourteen Dalai Lama. The shrines had no windows. The light came from the open door and from the few kerosene lamps. There were golden statues and framed holy texts. The visitors passed in silence under the watchful eye of the robed monks in attendance. Banknotes were scattered within the shallow enclosure around the pedestal of some statues. The tourist was curious, absorbing the details, breathing the incense. However, he gave up after the fourth chapel—they were so much alike, as if the inspiration had died after the first one. He walked back to the top terrace and took pictures of the landscape. Then he stood, just watching, the sun warm on his shoulders.

Later in the day he visited the Barkhor market. He haggled with street vendors and bought a doll in traditional Tibetan dress and a prayer mill. He walked at random, soaking in the hectic racket and the riot of colors.

Coming out of the bazaar, he paused in front of the Jokhang temple, taking in the pilgrims who, face down on the sidewalk, progressed body-length by body-length towards the wall of the monastery. Then he noticed the slim mattress that the pilgrims were using for each prostration. Those who had reached the wall were embracing it.

He observed the process for a while. His reasonable mind had difficulty adjusting to such fervor. He turned his back to the spectacle and walked to the taxi stand.

After a dinner of noodles and watery vegetables, he went back to his cold room, his mind still reeling from the mixed impressions of the day.

4

The monk was a strong believer, in kindness, in love of mankind, in wisdom, in enlightenment, in good deeds. He believed in sharing—friendship, wealth, jokes, mercy, anything worthwhile really. He loathed selfishness, greed, pretence, intolerance. He thought and professed that religion—any religion—was a channel for the spread and distribution of goodness.

He decided to be bold, once again.

The office of the Pangchen Lama, abbot of the monastery, wasn't accessible to the public, nor even to the novices who would hear the abbot's teachings and commands at the daily prayers. Only some privileged outsiders, most of them wealthy benefactors, would be shown in here. The large polished desk had a stack of files. The old monk noticed that the top one was labeled "Bank". A satellite phone was hooked to a smart-looking laptop. On the walls, between a wheel of life and holy writings, was a large photograph of the abbot, smiling, standing next to the fourteenth Dalai Lama. The abbot, plump and jolly like an earthly reincarnation of Lord Buddha, was leaning back in an elaborate desk chair, in a pose designed to impress.

The monk realized that, once again, his sixty years of age, his travels, thoughts and studies, would not impress this down-to-earth, or perhaps rather down-to-gold, blinkered administrator.

"Your Holiness, I attended the "jhator" of old Tsepak. We left his body on the consecrated peak and the birds started his sky burial before we left, all as prescribed. His family needs help now, though. His wife is old and crippled. Their children have long left for China and there has been no news from them. Tsepak was also supporting two sisters. They are now destitute. We have to help."

"You did well, my son," crooned the abbot. "I have received a report already. Tsepak's widow will receive 500 yuan tomorrow. Was that why you wanted to see me?"

The old monk smarted a little at being called "my son" by a man twenty years his junior. Yet years of humility took control. He had to go for it now.

"Your Holiness, 500 yuan is enough for her to live for two weeks. What then? There are dozens, hundreds of Tsepak in the villages. The monastery is rich in money and in people. Can we not provide more help to the communities? The villages need better schools, clinics, training in modern methods of cattle farming, and of crop growing. We could help with a cooperative society. And perhaps we could persuade the villagers to use the crematorium provided by the state, instead of leaving bodies in the open for the sky burial."

"Tenzin, Tenzin, my son, there you go again. For a start, the monastery is not rich. The donations we receive are barely enough to sustain our thousand monks and novices, their food and clothes, the heating in winter, the holy books, the maintenance of the buildings and support for the likes of Tsepak's family. Your concern for the community is commendable, but remember our vows: the three jewels of our life are the Lord Buddha, Dharma, the teachings and Sangha, the community. One should not exclude or even take precedence over the others.

"The welfare of the population is for the state to take care of. We can only guide people towards enlightenment. As for "jhator", you know very well the cost of the crematorium. There is no charge for alms to the birds. Fuel is not free. No, Tenzin, you must concentrate on praying to our Lord and review the teachings. You're a senior monk, you may not misguide the novices or mislead the people; their attention is fragile. Do not misguide them away from the middle way."

The monk sighed. He had lost already.

"Remember, Tenzin. We have had these talks before. You're an intelligent member of our congregation. You're welcome amongst us as long as you remain one of us. Help where you can, and as you may be instructed." With that the abbot signaled the end of the interview. There was a cold undertone to the dismissal.

The old monk straightened his back, bowed and walked out. The corridor outside was cold. Tenzin crossed a couple of mischievous novices, chasing each other. He sighed again.

5

"Qomolangma."

The tourist whispered the mouthful of unfamiliar syllables. Here was the holy mountain, the top the world — Mount Everest to foreigners. The sight of it alone was mind boggling. He was standing at the base camp, some 5,500 meters above sea level, ten kilometers away from it and still the mountain was towering over the landscape in a sparkling overwhelming mass. No wonder the Tibetans had made a goddess out of the place.

He examined the features, the Rongbuk glacier, the ridge that leads to the summit. He thought he could recognize the Hilary step, from this distance hardly a notch on the outline of the mountain, if that was it at all. His eyes followed the path to the west that had seen the demise of Mallory. He felt the urge that all men suffer before an inviting trial.

The tourist resisted the urging of the driver. He didn't want to go. He couldn't detach his sight from the radiant mountain. With the advancing afternoon, Qomolangma had taken on hues of shining gold. The cloud at the tip of Everest had grown into a fully-fledged stream of white plumes, flowing downwind for miles.

The tourist was out of breath in the thin air, his head light. Still, he had satisfied one unexplained aspiration and he rejoiced in the unique sight. He could stay there forever.

The driver pulled at his sleeve one more time, pointing at the setting sun.

"We have to go back, sir. It takes three hours to drive to Shigatse. We must leave."

It was getting seriously cold. Back in the car, he twisted in the seat to continue watching the luminous mountain through the rear window.

*

Past Tingri, the tourist noticed a desolate hilltop covered with lines of multicolored flags fluttering in the evening breeze. Several large birds were circling the summit. He asked the driver if there was a temple there.

"No temple, sir," was the curt reply.

"What is it then? What are the flags for?"

"Prayers, sir."

"Why are they there, then?" he insisted.

"Prayers for the dead."

"Up there?"

"Yes, sir. That place cemetery. For the dead."

"Do you mean people are buried up there?"

"No, sir. Not buried. Birds make burial."

The driver had answered, inserting long silences between his few words, unwilling to share Tibetan privacy with a foreigner. The tourist shrugged and went back to his reverie, staring at the endless panorama of mountains.

Nature was awe-inspiring, people were bewildering.

He mused for a while—irreverent as the thought was— about what to do in case of a bird's dropping on the windshield. What if it was a transmogrified version of the recently deceased cousin of his innkeeper on his way to nirvana?

6

The driver insisted that, in Shigatse, a visit to the Tashilhumpo monastery was a must. Tashilhumpo was the seat of the Pangchen Lama, second only to the Dalai Lama. A few hundred years ago, the monastery had boasted close to ten thousand monks. It still had a thousand today. The tourist wondered whether he should be impressed.

The monastery had the shape and layout of a large village with portals, chapels, houses, squares, streets and blind alleys. He wandered about for a while, very much on his own. At a fountain in a corner of a square, a monk was washing socks. A couple of tourists passed him by with smiles and bowed heads.

A large structure soared above the community. Its red wall rendering, gold trims and hefty pagoda roof made it the obvious focus of the convent. He walked into the place.

A sign at the entrance warned against photography. Again the interior was dark. He found a large golden statue of the Lord Buddha, showing off the perennial mild smile, surrounded by candles. He went around the statue, looking at the scriptures and paintings on the walls.

He came to another bulky figure, resting on a waist-high pedestal. A glass enclosure surrounded the base of the statue which rested in the lotus position. The space between the glass and the statue was filled with crumpled banknotes, about one foot deep. A shadow emerged from behind the glass case — an elderly monk who was evening out the surface of the donations with a rake, to spread the money uniformly and make room for further contributions. The monk, ankle deep in the cash, had tucked a corner of his robe in his belt to free his movements.

The tourist was engrossed by the unusual scene and gaped at the monk. The monk couldn't ignore him. He pushed his spectacles back to the top of his nose and, looking down at the foreigner below, inclined his head in greeting, all the while working the money. He then re-entered the darkness behind the statue. The tourist, still baffled, stood still and gazed at the banknotes. He figured that, as a minimum, there was a couple of million yuan in the "money-bed".

Back at the hotel he had an early dinner. Chinese food. No choice. He used to like Chinese cuisine. However, having been served it morning, noon and evening for five days in a row, he was craving a piece of bread. He asked the waiter. It was hopeless; the waiter didn't understand a word. The tourist tried to draw an illustration on a paper napkin. The waiter didn't understand. The tourist finished the rice and the soup.

He went out for a walk in the gathering dusk, hoping to find alternative sustenance at the supermarket he had spotted down the street. The shop was bright with neon lights. The shelves were stacked with products labeled in Chinese or Tibetan. Few were identifiable. He picked up a can and from the picture guessed that it contained noodles. He replaced the can and drifted along the displays. He went twice around the supermarket; no luck. Shoppers were looking at him with curiosity. He tried asking the till attendant. The girl shook her head with energy. Still no luck.

He felt a light pressure on his shoulder and turned around: a bespectacled shopper in a maroon robe was removing his hand.

"Can I help you?" asked the monk in clear English.

"With pleasure." The tourist was relieved to have communication. He asked, "Do they have bread in this shop?"

"You will not find bread in Shigatse. You could try biscuits."

The tourist looked at the monk, the face and the spectacles.

"You're from the monastery, right?"

"Yes I am. I saw you this afternoon."

"And you were tidying up the money in the chapel. Your monastery is very rich, it seems."

The monk relented with a cheerless smile. "Not as much as you would think. The abbot would tell you the costs of maintaining the buildings and the congregation."

The tourist and the monk chit-chatted for a while, two idle old men from worlds apart, yet with some like disposition.

"Anything else you would like to buy here?"

"If I were to buy a bottle of whisky, would you have a drink with me?" the tourist asked with a mischievous sparkle in his eye.

"Please forgive me for not sharing the drink with you, but I could keep you company with tea."

7

The tourist bought a bottle of Jack Daniels and a packet of biscuits. They walked back to his hotel and settled in the least drafty corner of the lounge. The monk warmed his hands around a glass of tea.

The tourist enquired how one would become a monk and what fulfillment that brought about. The monk obliged and recounted the early appeal of wisdom and enlightenment, perhaps the appeal of status and security as well, encouraged by his parents. Prompted by the tourist, he went on to describe his studies, his travels, the research, the meditation and the hope of nirvana. A waiter brought an electric heater, placing it in front of them. The heat and the warmth of the drinks made the old men stretch a bit in their seats. The monk explained the eight-fold path (Dhamachakra) and the Bodhisattva vows to attain the six perfections of giving, discipline, effort, meditation and transcendent wisdom. The monk was encouraged by the genuine interest of the tourist.

The tourist talked about his own religion, or at least that under which he had been brought up. He talked about his misgivings and doubts. He gave details of the rites he had seen elsewhere. He mentioned his personal search for the meaning of life and the existence of a grander scheme. He talked of his hope to discover something in Tibet.

The monk asked about the reasons of his past uncertainties. The tourist described the gap between the tenets of the religion he knew and the deeds of its priests. He commented on the soundness of the teachings and on the understanding of the common people. He shared his anguish at the tragedy of intolerance. His visit to Tibet was a further attempt to discover worth in spirituality and holiness in the human earthly jumble.

The monk invited more explanations. Then the tourist invited the monk's responses to his dilemma.

The monk paused. He turned away slightly from his companion and spoke in a low voice, as if to no-one in particular: "You have seen me displaying the donations of our people in the shrine, this afternoon. I do not like the duty and I do not like the show. However, the people of our country like it; giving alms to the monastery is part of their duty. The quantity is a measure of their faith, of their devotion. It is a measure of their progress towards illumination and enlightenment, perhaps." The monk didn't look up.

"Really?" said the tourist. "It seems to me that the people here could do with more money themselves and giving away the little they have is not helping their lives. I would say that they need their money more than the monastery."

"What matters is what they think. If it makes them feel good, then it's good for them. They have little else, you know."

"Do you say that the satisfaction of giving away makes up for the difficulties of having less? Is there not some perversion of values here?"

The sun went down. Their corner became dark. They kept silent for a while. The tourist then insisted gently: "Do you truly believe that your people understand religion and your teachings in any depth? And to the extent that they do, are they enlightened and better off for it?"

"You ask too many questions, my friend," answered the monk. "But I shall not take offence from your inquisition. You have a point that most people are simple. Their comprehension may be off the mark, so to speak, and may be close to superstition. Monasteries unfortunately not only take advantage of their lack of perception, but also perpetuate the condition."

The tourist persisted: "And if we assume that mental aptitude and proper education are available, would you say that the religious establishment will advance the lot of the people here? I'd like your honest opinion."

"Honest? Honest to whom? To an abbot who may still be too young? To myself who may be too old to care? To vows that may not have been given with full knowledge either way? To you whom I do not know? You demand much, my friend," was the reply.

The tourist refilled his glass. He was drinking the whisky neat.

"Did you ever drink whisky?" he asked.

"I did, in a previous life. Long ago, before my vows. I will have a glass now."

GLOSSARY

An explanation of some of the names and words used in the African and Arabian stories.

Swahili

Kansimba: village of the North Katanga province from where Major Schramme recruited youngsters to form what became the 10th Commando Battalion "Kansimba"
kasuku: sap similar to that from a pine tree, used for torches
kuja: come!, to come
kuna: there, over there (lingala)
Lumumba: first prime minister of independent Congo (assassinated 1961).
lupangu: fenced enclosure for animals or gardening
makanya: fork, also the nickname of my cook
munganga: doctor, by extension witch doctor, sorcerer
mutumbu: canoe, dugout
panga: machete
shamba: cultivated field
simba: lion, also war name of Mulelist rebels (Congo 1964)
sombe: vegetable similar to spinach
upesi: quickly
wapi?: where?

Arabic

dishdash: robe worn by Arab men on the Arabian Peninsula, usually white

gutrah: square piece of cloth, usually white or checkered, part of a man's headgear

salam aleikum: peace be with you

thobe: another word for dishdash

About the Author

Michel Gauthier graduated as a construction engineer from the Ecole Polytechnique of Brussels University. Contracting is a semi-nomadic profession which took him to Africa, the Middle East and the UK. It is also an adventurous activity which brought him, over a long career, into a number of unusual circumstances. Michel shares the resulting experiences, emotions, anxieties and exultations in true stories and tales that could be true.

Married with one son, Michel has settled in Thailand. He writes fiction and non-fiction.